LEVENMOUTH AT WAR

LILLIAN KING

ISBN NO: 0 9539839 8 6

Acknowledgements

I would like to express my gratitude to everyone who
contributed in any way to this book.
Special thanks go to
David Alexander, whose idea it was
The East Fife Mail
Levenmouth Regeneration Initiative
The staff of Methil Library and Methil Heritage Centre
Kirkcaldy Museum & Art Gallery
Fife Council Archives, Home Front Recall
William Hammond

LOTTERY FUNDED

Cover design by Belle Hammond
Typesetting, layout and design   by Windfall Books
Published by Windfall Books for
Levenmouth Regeneration Initiative
Printed by Nevisprint, Fort William

FOREWORD

COUNCILLOR DAVID J. ALEXANDER

This is a unique book. But so are the people whose experiences it describes and so are the communities in which they lived and died.

No other area of Britain, far less Scotland, is better suited to tell the story of the Second World War. Many areas have a mining tradition. Many coastal communities have docks. Many areas can boast a rural and urban mix, and many areas welcomed different nationalities during the war years. But Levenmouth combined them all - like no other.

This book, by well respected author, Lillian King depicts for the first time what the war years were like for the soldiers, sailors, airmen, merchant seamen, wives, children, miners, Poles, and munitions workers of Levenmouth. Much of it is told in their own words.

We realise that events like the sinking of the Royal Oak, Tunisia, Dunkirk, D Day, Arnhem and Burma were not just names in history. They all had a human impact, whether it was in Methil, Buckhaven or Kennoway, when the dreaded telegram arrived. We learn about the importance of Methil Docks and we hear first hand accounts of the raids and dogfights in the Forth.

The crucial role women played in WW11 is only now being recognised. This book adds to that knowledge. And there's the Home Front, rationing, blackouts, shelters, gas masks, school and barrage balloons.

But this is wartime and Levenmouth men died. And tragedy was never far away at home either; the mine explosion at West Wemyss that killed four miners, one a fifteen year old boy; the mine explosion in Buckhaven that took ten lives, eight of them children; the men that drowned in Methil Docks because of the blackouts; and the smallpox epidemic that claimed lives in 1942.

There are also stories of remarkable courage and endurance. Who was the Denbeath man who escaped from a POW camp in Italy, spent a year trying to get home, and when he did had a party in Denbeath Hall that was full of well wishers? Who was the Kennoway DCM holder who was pulled through the village with his family in a car with ropes? Who was the squaddie who arrived home in Methil from Dunkirk on the Saturday and was playing for Leven pipe band on the Sunday?

And there are other gems: A London War Weapons week raised a million pounds, but a similar event in Leven raised £125,000 in two days. A Buckhaven squaddie who used to work for Allen Litho produced the first British newspaper in Tunisia - it was published within twenty four hours of the Germans leaving. Jim Callaghan, who went on to become British Prime Minister, met up with the girls from Innerleven Laundry and danced in the Jubilee Hall.

A Flight Lieutenant from Methil was decorated as part of a crew that flew Churchill and the King on separate flights to North Africa. The famous German General Von Arnhim was captured by a tank crew who had a Methil man as driver.

This book is essential reading. The story has never been told before. Lillian has amassed a wealth of history, national and local, that will both inspire and shock contemporary readers. To the men and women who took part – "When will we see your likes again?"

CHAPTER ONE – 1939

'This morning, the British Ambassador in Berlin handed the German Government an official note stating that , unless we heard from them by 11 o'clock that they were prepared to withdraw their troops from Poland, a state of war would exist between us. I have to tell you that no such undertaking has been received, and that, consequently, this country is at war with Germany.'

This was how, on Sunday, September 3rd, 1939, Levenmouth, in common with the rest of Britain heard the news that the second world war had begun. Parliament had held its first Sunday sitting for over one hundred and eight years and, throughout the country, people switched on their radios to hear the Prime Minister, Neville Chamberlain, announce that Britain was at war with Germany.

The announcement was not unexpected. Since Hitler came to power in 1933, the build up of armaments production in Germany, and the increased power of its army, naval and air forces had been milestones to this moment. In January 1939, Hitler announced in a speech to the Reichstag that a war in Europe would lead to the annihilation of the Jewish race in Europe. In March, German troops occupied Czechoslovakia, and claimed Bohemia and Moravia. Less than a month later, Great Britain and France guaranteed armed help to Greece and Romania, should they be attacked by Germany or Italy, and formal Anglo-French guarantees were given to Poland.

In the summer of 1939, Hitler demanded that the so-called Danzig corridor be placed under German sovereignty. Poland refused, and at the end of August, German SS troops, dressed in Polish uniforms, pretended to attack a German radio station at Gliewitz, to convince the world that Poland was the aggressor nation, and to justify the coming invasion of Poland. On the first of September, the German naval training ship *Schleswig Holstein* fired the opening shots of World War II and shelled the Polish naval base at Westerplatte.

In the early hours of the morning, despite the knowledge that Britain and France were determined to defend Poland against German aggression, a full scale attack on Poland had been launched . German troops invaded Poland, supported by dive-bombers. The speed of the invasion gave it the name *Blitzkrieg*, or lightning war. It involved the massive use of tanks, motorised infantry and the airforce. The Polish armies were soon encircled or forced to retreat. At nine o'clock, England and France issued an ultimatum to Germany.

This final plea to Hitler to cease hostilities and withdraw from Polish territory was ignored and Britain had no choice but to declare war, but Britain and France were unable to intervene effectively on Poland's behalf. Germany's Blitzkrieg overran Poland from the west and on 17th September the country was invaded by the Soviet Union from the east. On September 27th,Warsaw surrendered and, two days later, Germany and the Soviet Union signed a treaty of friendship which partitioned Poland between them.

In Scoonie Church that third of September Sunday morning, a more than usually serious air prevailed, which was not decreased when the service was interrupted by an announcement that the air raid warning had sounded and the church had to be vacated. In St John's Church, the minister told his congregation that he was prepared to continue with the service but that anyone who wished to leave could do so. Only a very few did so.

Not everyone was concerned with the bigger picture, however. There were complaints about the Sunday calm being disturbed by the sound of planes when members of the Observer Corps were getting air experience.

That evening, people again gathered round their wireless sets to hear the King's broadcast to the Empire. He spoke of how the government had 'tried to find a peaceful way out of the differences between ourselves and those who are now our enemies.' He went on to say that we had been forced into conflict, to meet the challenge of a principle which, if it were to prevail, would be fatal to any civilised order in the world.

This principle would allow a state, in the pursuit of power, to disregard all treaties and solemn pledges, and in its simplest form meant the primitive doctrine that might is right would prevail. We had to meet the challenge, otherwise peoples would be kept in a bondage of fear and all hope of a settled peace, of security of justice and liberty among nations would be ended.

He went on to say that 'The task will be hard. There may be dark days ahead, and war can no longer be confined to the battlefield, but we can only do the right as we see the right......'

Preparations for the war had been going on for some time. Identity cards and gas masks were issued, the latter because of the fear of chemical warfare, and the use of poison gas that had been common in the first world war.

Scotland's evacuation scheme had been completed and nearly one hundred and seventy two thousand women and children were evacuated from what were seen as key targets for enemy attacks. Throughout Britain, about one and half million people, mostly children, were evacuated from the towns and cities to the countryside to avoid the expected air raids in the autumn of 1939.

Many city children from poor parents found themselves in strange surroundings and their hosts were sometimes startled by the gulf between them. For instance, many children were unaccustomed to a proper bathroom in the house. Working class children were billeted with middle class families, Protestants with Catholic and vice versa. City children were afraid of the country and missed the pictures and chip shops. For some it was a wonderful, if frightening, new life, for others a nightmare.

One of the biggest problems had been finding single accommodation for families of a mother and up to seven children, and in some cases, if suitable accommodation could not be found, families were sent home again. The quiet of the early months of war meant that many mothers took their children home again. However, as the threatened air raids began later in 1940, a second wave of evacuees went to the country. Some parents, usually the more affluent, sent their children to friends and relatives overseas for the duration of the war. Canada and America were popular destinations.

Fife had four thousand schoolchildren and it was impossible to staff schools adequately. Local schools were to remain closed till further notice, which caused problems as the children had been on holiday since the first week in July, and some were now 'running wild'. In fact the schools did not open till October 16th, because it was ruled that shelters must be provided for all children who could not get home within seven minutes of an air raid warning .

A church in Kinghorn was offered as a mortuary, should the need arise and all patients in hospitals in Cupar, St Andrews and Buckhaven were sent home. Only emergencies would be treated there, and women were asked to join the Civil Nursing Reserve. Evening classes were also suspended, cinemas and other places of entertainment closed and all functions where crowds were likely to gather were prohibited.

Orders for blackout were issued and householders and shopkeepers warned to darken houses and shops after dusk. Shops had to close early because of the blackout restrictions, but chemists were allowed to provide a restricted emergency service for those who could not attend doctor's surgeries during the day.

Street lighting was to be disconnected and emergency regulations for road vehicles brought into force. Air Raid Precautions (ARP) had been fully manned for some time and the first air raid siren shortly after the announcement of the outbreak of war gave them a chance to review these arrangements. Some air raid shelters had been built and preparations were made for trenches and dugouts. The Auxiliary Fire Service was mobilised and the fire stations put on twenty four hour duty. Regulations to prevent rises in coal prices, both wholesale and retail were put in place. Drastic reductions in railway services had been made all over the country. The coastal districts of Fife were very badly affected, but bus services continued as normal. Petrol rationing was to be introduced on September 16th, and people were warned that their property might be requisitioned.

In Fife, as in other parts of the country detachments of the local Black Watch Territorial Company mobilised and left to begin training.

The 302nd Battery R.A.T.A. was also mobilised and awaited orders. Newspapers reported a great number of applications to join the unit, but it was already at full strength.

Arrangements for the control of shipping at Methil Docks had already been made. A new Ministry of Shipping was set up to co-ordinate the activities of the merchant fleet. Plans for an organisation of this type had been drawn up before the war within the Board of Trade because of the expansion of departments dealing with shipping questions.

SS Athenia

The new Minister for Shipping was Sir John Gilmour, Bart; DSO of Montrave. A distinguished soldier and statesman, he commanded the Fife and Forfar Imperial Yeomanry during the First World War. First elected to the House of Commons in 1910 as Conservative member for East Renfrewshire, Sir John had since 1918, represented the Pollok

Division of Glasgow. He was Secretary of State for Scotland from 1932 – 1935. The first six months of the war are often referred to as the phony war but as far as shipping was concerned, it was real enough.

During both the First and Second World Wars deep waters around the western coast of Scotland made it impossible for the enemy to anchor mines to the sea bed, so ships laden with supplies and equipment for the allied forces congregated in this relatively safe haven as a gathering point forming convoys who were joined and protected by naval warships combating the heavy losses caused by Germany's U-boats.

In September 1939, the German navy had only forty three warships of destroyer size, against the Royal Navy's three hundred and ten, but they had three times as many submarines. German policy, therefore, was to destroy merchant shipping, cutting off essential supplies and bringing Britain to economic ruin. Britain's policy was that of protection, with merchant ships sailing in convoy with naval ships.

For the first months of the war, convoys ran from Methil to Bergen, but Bergen was captured by German troops on 9th April 1940.

In less than twenty four hours after the declaration of war, the Glasgow liner, *Athenia,* was torpedoed off the Irish coast. Among her fourteen hundred passengers were over three hundred citizens of the United States who had hurriedly left for home when war became imminent. The *Athenia* left Glasgow on Friday, the first of September, picked up more passengers at Liverpool and sailed for Montreal under wartime conditions, with portholes blacked out and passengers wearing life belts.

The first news of the attack came in a stark radio message reporting that the ship had been torpedoed and that passengers and crew, except those killed by explosion, had taken to boats and been picked up by various ships. Following the news of the attack, the offices of the shipping line in Glasgow and of the American Consulate were besieged.

One of the passengers was Robert Walker, of Montreal. A native of Leven, he had lived in Canada for thirty years, and after a holiday in Scotland, he left his son's home in Leven to return there, but ended up back in Methil.

He described what happened after the ship sailed from Liverpool. After supper on the Sunday night, he left the dining room and went on deck to have a smoke. He was standing at the stern when something struck the ship, near the stern, almost under where he was. There was no warning of an attack and he never saw any sign of a submarine.

'There was no mistaking that the ship was going down,' he said, 'and I hurriedly crept back to my cabin in total darkness to try and get some of my belongings, but I found it swamped out. I had to crawl back as best I could to the deck. They were manning the lifeboats and I was in the last boat to leave. The vessel was submerged at the stern and the water was up to my armpits by this time.'

To begin with, the sixty to seventy people - men, women and children - in the lifeboat had an anxious time.

'We had a great struggle to pull away from the sinking vessel. There didn't seem to be anybody in charge at first who could handle the boat. If the *Athenia* had gone down then, not one of us would have escaped, for the suction would have pulled our little vessel right under. After a bit, six of the crew got to the oars and we all gave a hand that could do so.'

It was nine o'clock at night when the lifeboat was launched and the survivors were not picked up until three in the morning. It was dark and cold and they were soaked to the skin when they were picked up by a Norwegian boat, which landed them at Galway the following morning.

After four days there, they were taken to Dublin, then Belfast and Glasgow before being taken home. In Robert's case, it was to Fife he returned, to his son's home in Aberhill. He described his experience as a grim ordeal and said he would not consider making the journey again till a proper system of convoy and protection was in operation.

The first British war ship to be lost in the war was HMS *Courageous*, an air craft carrier serving with the Home Fleet. On September 17th, she was torpedoed with the loss of five hundred and eighteen lives while on anti-submarine patrol off the coast of Ireland.

HMS Royal Oak

Levenmouth's first war casualties occurred on the night of October 13th, when the battleship *Royal Oak* was sunk by torpedoes from a German U-boat which had penetrated the navy's main anchorage in Scapa Flow in Orkney.

Of the eight hundred and thirty three men who died, one Henry Blyth came from Scoonie. The newspaper records the death of William Milligan from Methil, but according to official reports and the Imperial War Graves Commission register he is named as John McIsaac Milligan, son of William and Isabella Milligan from Methil. A third man John Farquhar, also from Methil, survived.

The *Royal Oak*, a Dreadnought battleship, had seen service in the first world war and was armed with the biggest guns ever fitted on a British naval vessel, capable of firing her huge shells onto targets eighteen miles away. By 1939, however, the *Royal Oak* could no longer keep up with faster, more modern ships, and she was posted to Scapa Flow to provide anti-aircraft cover. Ships in this area were thought to be quite safe from submarines because the narrow channels between the islands had been restricted by sinking block ships.

Shortly after midnight a German submarine, under the command of Gunther Prien, was lying off the east coast of Orkney and, taking advantage of a fast incoming tide, he slipped through a gap in the defences into calm waters. The *Royal Oak* was the only ship there, the others having been moved a few days earlier because of the fear of air attacks.

No-one expected a submarine attack and when the first torpedo struck, it was assumed it was an internal explosion and no alarm was sounded. The second attack resulted in three direct hits amidships, the *Royal Oak* began to list heavily to starboard, and within ten minutes she had disappeared beneath thirty metres of water. Almost two thirds of the ships crew died, and the three hundred and eighty six men who survived owed their lives to the skipper and crew of the *Daisy 2*. No more than one hundred feet long and fifteen feet wide, she managed in total darkness, to rescue them from the icy, oil covered waters of Scapa Flow. Some of the most severely wounded died later and were buried in the naval cemetery on the island of Hoy.

One of the survivors, Ken Conway, told his story.

'Friday October 13th was pay day and what we called 'quarterly settlement.' This was the occasion that the paymaster balanced your account and paid you any extra that came to light or took some off your pay if required. I had quite a bit extra as I had been uprated to signalman in that quarter. I know I played tombola that evening but I didn't win anything. Then it was off to bed, with my money belt tucked under the hammock mattress.

About one a.m. there was quite a loud bang and I jumped out of my hammock. Some ratings came running along the gangway and we asked what was wrong. They said they thought there was trouble in the paint store in the bows of the ship. It didn't seem particularly serious so we got back into our hammocks.

I hadn't been back in my hammock for more than ten minutes when there was a terrific bang and the ship shook violently and I could see a cloud of yellow smoke up forward. My feet hit the deck. I didn't give a thought to my money belt or getting dressed. I was on my way up the ladder from the mess deck to the port side gun battery. Through a mass of flames and smoke I could see a gathering of men where I knew there was a ladder leading to a passage outside the galley and then on to the upper deck. Someone at the bottom was helping men up the ladder and trying to calm them down. I don't know who it was, I think it was a chief petty officer. I was given an almighty push and before I knew it I was on the upper deck just about level with the second six inch gun barrel.

The ship had heeled over to starboard at the first explosion and now she started to tilt a bit more. I went over the guard rails and sat down on a small platform under the barrel of a six inch gun. Seconds later she began to tilt again and I got up and walked down the side and as the blister came up I pushed off into the waters of Scapa Flow. Had I jumped I would probably hit the blister as she capsized. I could see the ship's picket boat and I swam towards it. I clambered on board, little knowing it was already overcrowded. Before I knew it the boat capsized and I was back in the water. I swam a little way away and turned on my back. I could see the boat had righted itself and I swam to it again and clambered onboard once more. There was a lot of screaming from some of the men, I think they were mostly Maltese ships stewards.

There was a man standing up on the boat shouting 'Trim the boat' and attempting to push some of them off. The boat capsized again. Whether it sank or not on this occasion I don't know but I decided enough was enough and I struck out for where I thought the nearest land was on the starboard side of

Royal Oak. In daylight it hadn't seemed too far. I don't know how long I was swimming but I know I was getting tired when I bumped into what seemed a large piece of wood and I clung on to it using my legs to propel me towards what I thought was the shore.

After what seemed ages, although I couldn't see anything I heard a voice say, 'Here's another one' and I was grabbed and lifted out of the water on to the drifter *Daisy 2*. From the time I jumped out of my hammock until I was picked up I had been on my own and hadn't spoken to a soul. The *Daisy 2* carried on searching for more survivors until the skipper couldn't find any more or he was concerned for the safety of his boat and all on board. The *Daisy* made her way to the seaplane carrier Pegasus anchored nearby and disembarked the survivors. Here I was given a hot shower, most of the oil was removed and someone brought me a drink of rum, neat I think, and far more than the official ration. Clothing was provided either from the ship's store or by the ships crew giving up some of their own.

Later that morning I was transferred to a large liner, possibly the *Voltaire,* where I had a good breakfast. After the meal, I filed past a table at which were seated some officers recording name, rank, official number. They also wanted to know where I was at the time of the explosion, what did I think it was and how did I escape ... A brief visit to the clothing store and the Pay Office and then home for 14 days survivors leave. To say I wasn't scared would be a blatant untruth. For months after I would jump out of my skin at the sound of any bang, small or large. Even in the cinema I leapt out of my seat when a gun was fired.'

Divers were sent down to ascertain the cause of the disaster, and found several large doors tightly shut and bolted. Several portholes were open and survivors described how they managed to squeeze out of them to escape. Some managed to swim nearly a mile to the nearest cliffs, but a great many others perished in the freezing oil covered water. Sixty years later, traces of oil still seep from the upturned hull and rise to the surface.

Levenmouth at War

Ken went on to serve on HMS *Egret* escorting east coast convoys from Methil to Sheerness and back. They ran the gauntlet of E- boats and Stuka attacks coming under heavy air attack in August 1940 during the Battle of Britain, and, suffered numerous 'pepper pot holes' from the stukas. The *Egret* was based at Rosyth and left there in 1941 to join in the Battle of the Atlantic.

For the parents of Henry Blyth, who had served in the Navy for three years, the weekend the *Royal Oak* went down was filled with grim anxiety, made harder by the fact that their younger son had also chosen to join the Navy. He had to leave on the Sunday morning, before official news of his brother's death was received.

Milligan had served just over one year, and after his training ship period was over, he was transferred to the *Royal Oak*. His mother heard the news of the sinking when it was first announced on the BBC news bulletin. They had sat down to eat and switched on the news as a matter of course, she told the reporter

'I wasn't really paying attention until the voice started off 'The Admiralty regrets.... and then when he mentioned the *Royal Oak*, everything just seemed to slip away from me. It was terrible and then came that awful waiting, waiting, waiting for word. We got the telegram on Monday morning.'

There was a happier outcome for the Farquhar family, who also received a telegram, but it was to let them know their son was safe and well.

On 17th October, the press reported that fourteen German bombers had carried out a daring daylight raid on the Firth of Forth. A joint communiqué issued by the Admiralty, the Air Ministry and the Ministry for Home security said that:

'Today, October 16th between 9 a.m and 1.30 p.m, several German aircraft reconnoitred Rosyth. This afternoon, about half past two, a series of bombing raids began. These were directed at the ships lying in the Forth and were conducted by about a dozen machines. All the batteries opened fire upon the raiders and the Royal Air Force Fighter Squadron ascended to engage them. No serious damage was done to any of His Majesty's ships. A bomb glanced off the Southampton causing slight damage to her bow, and sinking the Admiral's barge and pinnace which were empty alongside.

This is the first hit which German air craft have made during the war upon a British ship. There were three casualties on board the Southampton and seven on the cruiser Edinburgh from splinters. Another bomb fell near the destroyer Mohawk, which was returning to harbour from convoy escort. This bomb burst on the water and its splinters caused twenty five casualties to the men on the deck of the destroyer which, like the others, is ready for sea.'

On that morning, a squadron of German bombers was on a mission was to search for and attack the battle cruiser HMS *Hood* which German intelligence believed was in the Forth making for Rosyth. A successful attack on the *Hood* would have provided a major boost for Nazi morale, but German intelligence had wrongly identified the battleship *Repulse* for the *Hood*, which was now being towed into dock at Rosyth. They attacked two cruisers, the *Edinburgh* and *Southampton*, which were lying at anchor a short distance east of the bridge.

Meanwhile Spitfires had been scrambled and the sky soon became filled with smoke from exploding anti-aircraft shells. One German bomber caught fire and went into a dive before crashing into the sea. Four of the crew were rescued by a fishing vessel, the *Dayspring*, but the body of their rear gunner was never recovered. The survivors were taken to the Military Hospital in Edinburgh Castle where they were treated for minor injuries.

A second wave of three bombers attacked, and three men on board the *Southampton* and seven on board the *Edinburgh*, were injured by flying splinters. The German Commander, Pohle, crashed into the sea about three miles out from Crail and, badly injured, was rescued by a trawler and transferred to the destroyer HMS *Jervis* and taken to the naval hospital at Port Edgar. Later in the afternoon, a merchant convoy with destroyer escort was entering the Forth, and one of the destroyers, HMS *Mohawk*, came under attack from another plane which dropped its two bombs, and strafed the full length of the Mohawk's decks with its machine guns. Fifteen of the *Mohawk's* crew were killed and at least ten others were wounded.

The destroyer's Commander, Richard Jolly was mortally wounded in the stomach, but he refused to leave the bridge, insisting that the other casualties be tended first. He brought the *Mohawk* into Rosyth at top speed and after berthing her, he was taken ashore, but died five hours later. Jolly was posthumously awarded the medal of the military division of the Order of the British Empire for his gallantry.

A number of other skirmishes took place, but by about four o'clock, the remaining raiders had either left or had been driven off. Only slight damage had been caused to the cruisers *Southampton* and *Edinburgh* and the destroyer *Mohawk*, which were all still ready for sea. The air raid did have the effect of causing a number of naval vessels to be moved away from the Forth, to a safer haven in the Firth of Clyde. Many accounts of this first Luftwaffe raid describe it as the attack on the Forth Rail Bridge, which was clearly not the case.

There were eye witness accounts of the raid. At Dalmeny Station at the south end of the Rail Bridge, a train was halted at the time of the attack and the passengers asked if they wished to alight. Most elected to stay on board, and as the train made its way slowly across the bridge, the passengers were given a grandstand view of the action.

Richard Smith, a Buckhaven businessman, and his brother Robert were passengers on the 2.30 ferry from North Queensferry to Hawes Pier when they saw an aeroplane appear from the south side of the bridge. The ferry captain thought there was something wrong with the engine as it appeared to be making a terrible noise.

'It appeared to me,' said Richard, 'to be more like gunfire. The plane soared into the sky and it was out of sight for a few minutes before it swooped down and dropped two bombs. The plane disappeared, then returned and dropped another two bombs, this time on the south side of the Southampton. The Southampton opened fire and the raider was beaten off.'

Just over a week later, William Duthie from Methil died when the *SS Orsa* was blown up and sunk in the North Sea after, it was thought, striking a mine. His work mate Alexander Watson, also from Methil, was rescued with other members of the crew after clinging to wreckage for six hours. Both men were firemen on the *Orsa,* which had a crew of twenty, and this was Duthie's first voyage on the vessel, having joined it just before it left Methil the previous week. William Duthie, who was thirty nine and unmarried, didn't stand a chance, Watson said, because he was on duty at the time of the explosion. The ship's boilers were blown up and he was working below.

Watson gave a graphic account of his own ordeal:

'I was on duty from midnight to four a.m. and after being relieved I retired to my bunk. I was enjoying a smoke before going off to sleep when suddenly there was a terrific explosion and I was thrown against the side of my bunk. My head came into violent contact with it and the blow temporarily dazed me. After things began to get a little clearer, I rushed up on deck. Everything was in complete darkness and we did not know what had happened, but the ship took a heavy list and began to sink rapidly. I assisted other members of the crew in an attempt to lower one of the lifeboats. We managed to get one end into the water, but the other end was caught in the davit owing to the angle at which the ship was lying. The lifeboat was drawn under the water and we had to jump clear to avoid being drawn under with it.'

With three other men, he managed to grasp a piece of wreckage and, with the help of Second Mate Goldie from Rosyth, who kept their spirits up when they felt like letting go, they survived for six hours till they were picked up by a destroyer.

Watson's brother William also had a lucky escape. He and James Egan, also from Methil, were crew members of the *Carmarthen Coast,* which foundered during an explosion in the North sea. Both were off duty when the whole ship shuddered from stem to stern with the force of the explosion. As quickly as they could, they dashed on deck and helped to launch the lifeboat. Fortunately it was daylight which made the launching of the boat easier.

Watson described what happened next.

'After the boat had pulled away from the side of the ship, we saw McDonald, the chief engineer, crawling along the deck. He had obviously been knocked out by the explosion and I think he must have come to sufficiently to drag himself on to the deck. I don't know what his thoughts were when he saw the lifeboat had left the ship but he crawled to the side and we shouted to him to throw himself into the water. The ship was sinking fast now and McDonald was obviously not able to get on his feet. He just rolled over the side into the water. We got a rope to him and dragged him aboard the lifeboat. Just after that, the ship disappeared. I think she would go down in about eight minutes.'

Methil seaman William Smith was a member of the crew of the British cargo steamer *Glen Farg* when the vessel was attacked and sunk by a German U-boat. Wounded in the head, he survived twenty eight hours in a small boat, tossed by heavy seas.

'Everything was over so quickly we hardly knew what had happened,' Smith told the press, 'We heard a couple of warning shots and, after the ship had been stopped, the German commander gave us time to leave. Our commander tried to put out an SOS but the sub crew evidently jumped at what was happening and promptly sent over another shot, intending, no doubt to put our aerial out of order. That shot all but cost me my life. I was standing on the lifeboat deck along with three other firemen and Davie Cooper, the donkeyman. There was a sudden crack of fire and Cooper fell to the deck. I felt a stinging pain in the side of the head and I found I had been wounded. Two other men were struck, but Cooper was the most seriously wounded.'

They managed to get two boats away and Cooper was

placed in one, but despite the efforts of his mates, he died about twelve hours later. Conditions were bad and getting worse, Smith expected the boat to founder, and they had begun to give up hope, when they sighted a destroyer approaching. They had been adrift for twenty eight hours when they were picked up. They were taken to a British port before being allowed home, where Smith made a good recovery from his injuries.

Another lucky escape was reported, this time by three German seamen. They were landed in Methil after being picked up by a trawler, after being adrift for six or seven days.

The men had been on board a ship which was being held in Kirkwall to be searched for contraband, and were told they would be interned. They believed they would be shot so, in desperation, they made their escape, hiding in one of the ship's lifeboats till heavy cloud enabled them to slip away unseen. They launched the life boat and rowed out into the open sea, confident that a U-boat would rescue them or that they could navigate their craft to the German coast.

Once clear of land, they hoisted a sail but they were afraid that they'd be sighted by passing British ships. When ships appeared on the horizon, they pulled down the mast and lay on the bottom of the boat. The men claimed to have got to within sixty miles or so of the Danish coast, but a strong easterly wind sprang up and weakened by several days' exposure, they could not battle against the wind, and began to drift away from land again.

At one point, the boat was capsized and the sailors were flung into the sea, but two of them managed to grab the upturned boat and right it. It took fifteen minutes for them to man handle the third man aboard, sails and oars were gone, their drinking water was salted and they had no food.

Eventually, the boat was swept back towards May Island, and they were picked up by a trawler and taken to Methil. They probably owed their lives to the fact that the boat was equipped with buoyancy tanks which kept it afloat. When picked up, they were in an exhausted condition, but recovered sufficiently to be handed over to the military authorities for internment.

In the summer of 1939, with war imminent, the German pocket battleship *Graf Spee* put to sea to await instructions. Immediately war was declared, those instructions were to find and destroy British merchant ships. By the end of the year, *Graf Spee* had sunk ships totalling over forty thousand tons. So successful was she that special 'hunting forces' were created to find and destroy her.

On December 2nd, the freighter *Doric Star* was captured off the coast of Africa but was able to transmit a signal identifying *Graf Spee* as her attacker. James Hutton of Leven who became a prisoner on the *Graf Spee* gave an account of what happened when the *Doric Star* was attacked by the German battleship.

'I was having a smoke on deck when I heard the bang of a shot going off and saw some splinters and shrapnel falling around. I jumped up and a piece of shrapnel fell at my back where I had been sitting. I picked it up but it was red hot and I quickly dropped it. Somebody remarked that I should keep it as a memento but I said, 'No fear. It's too hot to handle.'

About a couple of minutes afterwards there was another shot and the battleship came over the horizon. She must have been about twelve miles away when the first shot was fired. Our engines were stopped but we were still sending messages though we were receiving orders to stop wirelessing.

In about fifteen minutes a boarding party came alongside and we were given ten minutes to collect blankets, a plate, cup, knife and fork before being transferred to the battleship. A German officer told me to take one of the small boats...I was ordered to pull away and they started to sink the ship. When we pulled alongside the battleship, I saw the name *Deutschland* but knew she couldn't be because the *Rawalpindi* had been sunk two days before and the *Deutschland* couldn't have got to this spot so quickly. We all got on board safely and no-one was hurt....'

Hutton obviously believed that the *Rawalpindi* had been

sunk by the *Deutschland* but he was not the only one to wrongly identify the ship. Captain Kennedy of the *Rawalpindi* was informed that the *Deutschland* was in his area and warned to avoid combat because that would be suicidal. When a ship was spotted, Kennedy thought it was the *Deutschland* and sent a report to this effect. In fact the German battleship had developed engine trouble and had to return home for repairs. She was replaced by the battle cruiser *Scharnhorst*, which approached quickly, cutting off *Rawalpindi's* line of escape, signalling them to 'Heave To' and firing warning shots. Kennedy ignored them, and the signal to abandon ship. He opened fire but *Rawalpindi* had only eight obsolete six inch guns to *Scharnlorst's* eighteen eleven inch, longer range weapons. A lifeboat with forty men was lowered but turned turtle and hit the water upside down. Other boats were swamped when the *Scharnhorst* swung hard about, but she returned to pick up the thirty eight survivors. Two hundred and thirty eight men died. The crew of the *Doric Star* were more fortunate, as Hutton reported.

'The room where I was put along with twenty eight officers, already had fifteen officers from another ship. The room was only about seventeen by twenty one by seven feet, and next day another eight prisoners were crushed in when the *Graf Spee* sunk *the Tiaora.* That meant fifty one in a room meant to hold fifteen. Four days after our capture, *Graf Spee* made contact with a supply ship and one hundred and sixty prisoners were transferred. That made three hundred and thirty on board that ship. I consider myself lucky not to be transferred to that ship.

'All day the *Graf Spee* refuelled, and next morning she sank the *Streonshalh.* We had an idea we were somewhere off the South American coast. Then she met the *Exeter* about 5.30 a.m.

We were locked in a room on top of the magazine but we knew something serious was afoot because the signals were much more elaborate than before. From six to eight, the battle was fierce, we heard and felt two or three good hits and shrapnel fell into our room, but no-one was hurt. There was a considerable amount of alteration in course and some time later it became evident the *Graf Spee* was running away. There was a long lull then came two or three shots in the afternoon. We heard later that these had come from the *Ajax* who had broken through the smoke screen and got six direct hits before *Graf Spee* could return fire. Things were quieter after that.

We played cards and went to sleep. We were wakened by a German officer who told us we were in Montevideo. 'For you the war is over. Tomorrow you go ashore.'

On arrival at Montevideo, *The Graf Spee's* commander Captain Langsdorff, released the merchant navy crews he had on board, and all spoke highly of their treatment by him. Of the nine ships sunk, not one crew member had been killed. The warship was not badly damaged and so could not be allowed to remain in a neutral port. Langsdorff was led to believe that five British ships, including an aircraft carrier, would have to be faced when he left port. His only alternative was to scuttle the ship to prevent it falling into enemy hands. The *Graf Spee* left with a skeleton crew and stopped three miles out of Montevideo harbour. Explosives had been set to go off after the crew members had abandoned the ship, which was still burning four days later.

Hutton described what happened. They had been told by German sailors that the ship wouldn't sail, but then a shout went up that *Graf Spee* was making for sea. As they watched, 'she went up like a flash and for a long time there was as brilliant a display of pyrotechnics as I have ever seen.'

The sailors from the *Doric Star* had seen the end of the *Graf Spee*, pride of the German fleet but, locked on board they had been unaware that, on December 13th, she was fighting her last battle, which would go down in history as the Battle of the River Plate.

CHAPTER TWO - 1940

The supply ship which took off the one hundred and sixty prisoners would have been the *Altmark*, which would also make her mark in naval history.

The *Altmark* was an unarmed supply ship and was assigned to the *Graf Spee* to support the battleship during her raids in the North Atlantic. Sailors rescued from ships sunk by the *Graf Spee* were transferred to the *Altmark* to be taken to prisoner of war camps in Germany. After the transfer of prisoners in December, the *Graf Spee* headed for South America and the *Altmark* spent some more time in the North Atlantic before heading for home. As a naval auxiliary ship she could legally claim freedom from search by foreign forces. On February 16th, 1940, the British cruiser *Arethusa* with the 4th Destroyer Flotilla intercepted the *Altmark* off the south coast of Norway. Two small Norwegian warships escorted the *Altmark* and they warned the British ships not to interfere with the supply ship.

The commander of the 4th Flotilla, Vian, received orders from Winston Churchill at the Admiralty to board the *Altmark* even though she had taken refuge in Norwegian waters. An offer was made that the she could go to Bergen under escort to be searched. However, when the destroyer *Cossack* tried to pull alongside the much larger *Altmark*, the supply ship attempted to ram the *Cossack*. In doing so, all the *Altmark* succeeded in doing was to run aground. In the last major boarding action to be fought by the Royal Navy, British sailors rushed aboard her and, after some hand to hand fighting, freed the two hundred and ninety nine merchant sailors who had been held on board. The *Altmark* was re-floated at high tide and continued to Germany, minus her prize.

The Norwegians were angry that their neutrality had been infringed and did not want to be dragged into a European war. There had been open discussions between Britain and France about the possibility of occupying Scandinavian countries to prevent them falling into German hands, and but shortly after what became known as 'The Altmark Incident', Germany invaded Norway and Denmark. It is possible that this was a previously planned strategy and was not connected to 'The Altmark Incident', but the capture of nearly three hundred merchant seamen so early in the war would have been a tremendous propaganda coup for Germany.

The incident was greeted with joy in Britain and the legality of it was never questioned. The Norwegians were angered by what they saw as a blatant infringement of their neutrality, as the *Altmark* was in Norwegian waters at the time of the boarding. Hitler was furious. What should have been a propaganda coup for Germany turned out to be the opposite. Within days, he ordered plans for the invasion of Norway to go ahead.

Norway was strategically and economically important to both Germany and the Allies. Control of its coastline could either help Britain to strengthen its blockade, or provide Germany with suitable bases for its navy. It was also a vital outlet for Swedish iron ore, an essential part of Germany's war economy. Hitler decided to pre-empt an Allied move and on March 1st 1940, ordered the seizure of Norway and in the process, Denmark. German troops invaded Norway by sea and air on April 9th, seizing key locations while the Luftwaffe took control of the air. Unable to prevent the invasion, the Royal Navy nevertheless inflicted significant losses upon the German surface fleet. British, French and Polish units were sent to assist the Norwegians but their efforts were uncoordinated and poorly planned. They failed to dislodge the Germans, and withdrawal followed. The last units left Narvik in June 1940.

On February 18th,1940 HMS *Daring* was torpedoed and sunk off the Pentland Firth by a German submarine. *Daring* was escorting a convoy from Bergen to Methil. There were only five survivors, and a hundred and fifty seven men were lost . Later in the month, William Christie from West Wemyss claimed to have the luck of a cat. He escaped from the *Baron Ailsa* which sank in the North Sea after an explosion.

'So quickly did the ship go down - she was out of sight in two minutes – I didn't even have time to put a life belt on. The mate stood on the ship's side till it disappeared under him and as he jumped for the lifeboat he realised that the painter rope was still holding it to the ship. He sliced through it. If he hadn't done so the boat, and all in it, would have been dragged under.'

The captain tried to swim to the lifeboat but he was struck on the head with a piece of floating wreckage and was dead when they picked him up.

At home, the year began badly with a New Years Day announcement that two million men between the ages of twenty and twenty seven were to be called up. Nineteen year olds would have to register and be called up at twenty, and twenty six year olds had to register. Within a few weeks, the conscription age had gone up to thirty six.

There was a row over a pay increase for the colonel in charge of ARP. By paying him an extra £100.00 a year , it was claimed, they were sounding the death knell for the voluntary service. Why should he be paid to maintain enthusiasm of the men who were doing it for nothing. The wardens were responsible for ensuring that blackout regulations were adhered to but on one occasions their cry of 'Get that b.....light out' was unavailing. The night sky over Methil was lit up as a Danish steamer went on fire as she was taking on coal,

Food rationing began in January, with allowances of four ounces each per person per week of butter and bacon and twelve ounces of sugar. Obtaining any of these food from the Irish Free State, which of course was neutral, was punishable by six months imprisonment. On a lighter note, the BBC began broadcasting the Forces Programme, allowing it to play dance music on Sundays. The corporation had banned this since broadcasting began in 1922.

Lord Haw Haw, in his regular propaganda broadcasts from Germany gave three talks on books by A.J. Cronin. *The Stars Look Down*, based on a mining community, was used to denounce the way the mining industry was organised and run.

The result was perhaps not what he had hoped for – the library was inundated with requests for the books. People were used to propaganda by this time. After the first raid on the Forth on October 16th 1939, Haw Haw reported, much to the annoyance of the Rosyth ladies who watched the raid, that peasants in Scotland were waving to the pilots. Laura Wilson was one of the watchers.

'The planes were so low, we thought the pilot must be sick because he was leaning out over the side of the plane, but he must have been taking photographs, because that night Haw-Haw came out with this about the Scottish peasants. My neighbour said, 'That's us he's talking about.' When all the street signs and direction labels were taken down, he said we'd be as well taking the labels off strawberry jam so they wouldn't know what kind it was.'

Frank Rankin also remembers the propaganda broadcasts .

'We always listened to Lord Haw-Haw. I considered him to be the second best comedian to Tommy Handley. One night we were wakened up in the middle of the night by three 'crumps', obviously bombs. The next day Lord Haw-Haw told the world that The Royal Scot had been bombed making its way through Fife.

Being a railway enthusiast I said, 'Away you go – the Royal Scot is an LMS engine and the LMS doesn't come through Fife.'

The next day my father told us that a German bomber had spotted the light from the firebox of a Wemyss Coal Company pug engine and dropped three bombs, one at 'The Maw' on the north side of the Standing Stone Road, another in a field and another on the east side of Michael Colliery. The pug engine and crew were unharmed and some wag wrote 'The Royal Scot' on the side of the engine with chalk.'

Conscientious objectors were quite a problem for the authorities. The press reported that they were to attend tribunals, and added that in Germany they'd be in concentration camps. Tribunals, it said, were fair minded as a rule but there were occasional cases of prejudice, for example 'when a member of a simple minded sect known as Jehovah's Witnesses' was refused exemption.

Meat rationing began with adults allowed one shilling and ten pence worth, and children half that amount. This was about the equivalent of one pound weight of meat per week. The great dig for victory started and every week the newspapers published recipes on how to make the most of rations, with pickled eggs and sausage pies.

On April 3rd, the death of Sir John Gilmour from a heart attack was announced. He was only sixty three. The following week, the war took a back seat for a spell as a new chapter of the history of Methil church was begun with the laying of the foundations stone of the new Innerleven East Church. But not for long – all the churches in the area responded to the King's call for a national day of prayer, the miners gala day was cancelled and miners asked to give up their gala day holiday as coal represented the production of guns, shells, tanks and aeroplanes. Wemyss miners were asked to produce three thousand more tons of coal per week.

In May, the Amalgamated Engineering Union agreed that women should be allowed to work in munitions factories, and German and Austrian men between the ages of sixteen and sixty were interned. No German or Austrian was allowed to enter restricted areas without permission, and aliens of other nationalities living in these areas had to report to the police every day. They were not allowed to use bicycles or cars or go out between the hours of eight in the evening and six in the morning. Over the whole country about eleven thousand people were affected, and were either detained or had their movements restricted.

One of those affected, a Methil girl married to a German, was home on holiday when war was declared. She was ordered to be interned, could not communicate with her husband, and was not allowed to travel more than five miles from her home so she couldn't even take a bus into Kirkcaldy.

On May 13th, Churchill gave his 'Blood, sweat and tears speech,' and Anthony Eden appealed for men between the ages of seventeen and sixty five, who were not already engaged on military service, to form anti-paratroop units to guard local installations of importance. A Professor Haldane asked for surface workers at the pit head to be armed in order to deal with German parachutists. He claimed that an incendiary dropped down a mine shaft could kill up to a thousand men.

Women were to be allowed to work part time in munitions so men could be released for the forces, and conscientious objectors were to work on the land. Nurses, auxiliaries, and domestic workers to staff the new emergency hospitals, were needed. Thirty thousand women had registered with the Civil Nursing Reserve throughout the country, and they would be given first aid and home nursing courses, then two weeks practical work in hospital.

Anderson shelters had to be built according to regulations, covered with fifteen inches of soil at the top and thirty inches at the sides. If they didn't comply with the rules, they would be removed and penalties imposed. In fact, these shelters were totally unsuitable for their purpose. Built below ground level, they were flooded every time it rained.

It was forbidden to carry portable radios in cars and any car with a radio installed had to have it removed and dismantled. The ringing of church bells was prohibited, except as a warning that enemy troops were invading the country.

The threat of invasion was very real. On 10th May, 1940 the Germans unleashed a series of devastating and audacious operations against neutral Holland and Belgium, and at the same time Italy declared war on Britain and France. The Dutch army capitulated on 15th May and despite fighting for three weeks against overwhelming odds, Belgium was forced to surrender at midnight on May 27th.

Some of Britain's finest troops had been beaten back to the beaches of Dunkirk, and were saved by the armada of little boats which took them off.

The battle of Dunkirk lasted from around May 26th to June 4th and a large force of British and French troops was cut off by the German armoured advance to Calais. Around three hundred thousand British and French soldiers were squeezed into a seven mile wide area with their backs to the sea and facing the Germans, with not enough fire power or air support to win the battle. The beach at Dunkirk was on a shallow slope so no large boat could get near to the actual beaches where the men were and attempted rescue operations were only partly successful.

Smaller boats were needed to take on board men who would then be transferred to larger boats based further off shore. A call went out to civilians to provide shallow draught vessels and was answered by a fleet of about nine hundred private ships, fishing boats and pleasure craft. It is thought that the smallest boat to make the journey across the Channel was the *Tamzine* - an eighteen foot open topped fishing boat now on display at the Imperial War Museum, London. Within nine days, most of the soldiers were rescued – many of them to return within days to the battlegrounds of France.

After the French surrender, some French troops returned home but others chose to join the Free French in Britain and continued to fight. The soldiers covering the last stages of the retreat fell into German hands, were taken prisoner and started on what became known as The Great March. This started in France and ended in some cases in Poland, because Germany did not have enough prison camps to put them in.

One of the luckier ones was Private Robert Swan of Methil, described as 'one of the battle stained, bedraggled but defiantly determined British Tommies facing death in Flanders.' He arrived home on a Saturday and took his place in Leven Pipe Band on Sunday. Private Swan and his friend Private W. Somerville had worked together in Methil Co-op, olunteered together, were in the same unit and in the same fighting retreat from Brussels to Dunkirk. They came back to England on the same warship and travelled home together.

Private Robert Simpson also had a remarkable escape. His unit ran into a German advance party on the outskirts of Calais and there was a terrific encounter with overwhelming odds.

Simpson and others fought their way to the sea front and took shelter under a pier where they crouched for several hours till a naval cutter came alongside and they were able to jump aboard. Others were not so lucky with wounds of varying seriousness. Two of the three Alexander brothers from Denbeath, serving with the Royal Artillery, were wounded.

Wilfred Jamieson from Methilhill told how he escaped from France.

'We were sent out to France and had taken up positions in front of the Maginot Line when the big advance took place. A shell burst close to where I was standing and I was hit with shrapnel in both legs. Along with other wounded, I was taken to a hospital, which was heavily bombed by the Germans.

Members of an American Volunteer Corps came into the hospital and asked if I was able to make a dash for the south of France. I was carried to a motor ambulance and later found refuge in a large mansion house where we were well treated for a few days.'

The Italians were searching houses for refugees and the owner was frightened of what would happen if soldiers were found, so it was decided to make a bid for Spain. The men were smuggled on to a goods train but were stopped by a French policeman. At police headquarters his chief didn't seem to know what to do with them. He gave them food and money and told them to go.

'We picked up a young English lad whose parents had escaped when the big push came, and we hitch hiked on trains for four days. We crossed into Spain, got to a port and got aboard a ship.'

There was to be no let up for the country, though. On 18th June, Churchill gave his famous 'This was their finest hour' speech and warned that the Battle of Britain was about to begin. While it was raging, it didn't seem to have any noticeable effects on Levenmouth area, apart from the weekly publication of casualty lists. The whole country, though, was at times under red or yellow warning, with small raids over many areas. In August the whole of Britain was declared a defence area, and Civil Defence Volunteers were asked for. Stirrup pumps for tackling incendiary blazes were based at central points.

Entire families answered the call to arms, even when not strictly obliged to. Five Leven brothers, now resident in Canada, all joined the colours but a sixth, who had served in the first war, was deemed unfit for duty.

On June 22nd, France signed an armistice with Germany, German troops occupied northern and western France and the collaborating Vichy government was set up in the south-east. By the end of the month, German forces had landed in the Channel Islands, the only part of the British Isles to be occupied by enemy troops.

U-boat bases were set up in Brittany, and submarines no longer had to make passage north of the British Isles to reach the Atlantic and have access to the all-important shipping lanes to and from the USA. With the occupation of so many Norwegian, Danish, Belgian, Dutch, and French ports, the German navy was in a position to control the seas of northern Europe. Great Britain was now even more isolated and in one month alone allied shipping of more than 350,000 tons were lost to U-boats.

During the war, merchant ships, as many as two hundred on one day, were collected into convoys and lay off Methil. In June, just before Italy entered the war against Britain, Frank Rankin recalled seeing two large ships with the Italian Flag painted on their sides.

'Our house overlooked the sea, and looking out we saw a small ship coming out from Methil docks. Looking through binoculars we saw it was filled with armed sailors. The ship went alongside one of the Italian ships and the sailors went on deck.

The other Italian ship tried to escape, raising its anchor and sailing for the mouth of the Forth but it had to turn back because it needed a pilot to take it through the minefield at the mouth of the Firth of Forth. The two ships were taken over by the Royal Navy.'

People not directly involved were more concerned with mundane details of day to day living. Milk was provided cheaply for mothers and children, and free for families on limited incomes; margarine, fat and tea were rationed and iced cakes banned. Bread could no longer come in eighty five different shapes, bakers now had a choice of only four, and standard loaves of one pound were the rule to economise labour and reduce waste. In Scotland, however, probably because of the tradition of half–loaves, one pound twelve ounces was the standard weight.

Twenty nine allotments had been allocated in the burgh, but vandalism was rife and an appeal was made to parents to prevent wanton damage to public property. The Home Office banned fireworks, and kite and balloon flying.

An unusual 'Kill' was reported. The cargo vessel, *SS Highlander*, steamed into port with a Heinkel seaplane draped across her stern. The ship had just survived a bombing attack and the aircraft turned to rake her with machine gun fire, but was hit by the ship's gunners. It crashed into the sea, but immediately another aircraft turned up and dropped bombs which also missed their target, and it was also caught by machine gun fire. Losing height, its port wing hit the *Highlander's* port lifeboat and swung round on the poop deck where it caught fire. The ship's crew put out the fire and took its trophy home.

Ships continued to be sunk, some carrying coal, others pit props necessary for the mining industry. Others carrying human cargo were also destroyed. Many ships carrying internees were lost at sea by enemy torpedoes. After the outbreak of war in September 1939, known Nazi sympathisers were rounded up. This was the start of a campaign which lasted to mid-1940 by which time eight thousand aliens, including refugees who had fled Nazi Germany to escape persecution, had been gathered into camps to be deported to the Dominions.

This harsh policy was gradually relaxed after the sinking of the SS *Arandora Star* by a German U-boat in July 1940, with the loss of over eight hundred internees. This disaster led to vigorous protests about the British internment policy, which was changed to internment of enemy aliens in camps in Britain only.

The *Arandora Star* had left Liverpool for Canada on June 30th, 1940 and survivors described their experiences.

'The ship had the appearance of a troop carrier, being painted battleship grey and having the rear promenade decks and the lower decks boarded up completely. All portholes were boarded up shutting out all daylight and the ship was armed. The boarded up promenade decks were separated from the other parts of the ship by double fences of barbed wire reaching from floor to ceiling. The only means of communication between the aft and forepart and to the boat-decks was through the lower cabin gangways which were closely guarded by sentries.'

Accommodation was in two and three berth cabins with four and five men to each cabin, two in bunks, others sleeping on the floor on palliasses, or in the ship's ballroom aft, where some had palliasses, others slept on the bare floor with no blankets. Lavatory accommodation for over two hundred men consisted of four WCs and four washbasins. The internees were only allowed to enter these in small groups closely guarded by sentries. The *Arandora Star* carried fourteen lifeboats, which on average held fifty to sixty people each, and a number of life rafts. There was no official issue of lifebelts, but belts of various designs were lying about and it was left to everybody to provide himself with such a belt if thought necessary. No instructions whatever were given for the possible event of being shipwrecked; no boat drill was held, no one was instructed in the proper use of a lifebelt, and no instructions were given as to how to proceed in the event of an emergency.

The ship sailed without escort or convoy and on Monday July 1st she was pursuing a short but continuous zigzag course. All outer lights were extinguished and the ship was absolutely dark. With the numerous sentries on deck and the guns silhouetted against the sky the ship had the definite appearance of an armed merchantman troop carrier. Just after seven the next morning, a torpedo hit the *Arandora Star* below the waterline, shaking her by a violent explosion. The light in the cabins and inner gangways went out, and apparently the electrical installation was put out of order immediately; no alarm was sounded and whoever was able to do so went from cabins and living quarters to the decks to reach one of the lifeboats.

Everyone tried to save his life as best as possible. There was no visible attempt made, however, to organise the evacuation of the ship, but the last six boats were lowered in good order, and filled almost to capacity; four others were lowered safely, but with very few survivors in them, almost exclusively British soldiers. Many rafts, boards, benches, etc, were thrown into the water, and people who could not get to the boats jumped overboard and hung on to them as best they could. Some people, already in the water and making for the rafts, were injured by other rafts thrown down. Many sick and elderly people stayed on board and went down with the ship. The lifeboats were in poor condition, and two of the motor boats had only empty petrol canisters.

Several boats were lowered with less than ten occupants but all did their best to pick up survivors from the water and from wreckage pieces to which they were clinging. They kept together as best they could within a short distance from the *Arandora Star*. The ship broke in two by a second, apparently a boiler, explosion, before she finally sank about 7.40 a.m.

It was a dreadful sight as many people were still on the upper decks holding on to the railings. At about 2.30 p.m, the destroyer *St. Laurent*, approached and at once started to take on board survivors off the rafts, while its motor-launch picked up survivors who were swimming in the water or clinging to the rafts.

On board the destroyer everything was done to make survivors as comfortable as possible. Many were exhausted, from up to seven hours in the water, and black from bilge or fuel oil; those from the lifeboats suffered from cold and exposure, as they were mostly in pyjamas. Hot rum, cocoa and biscuits, dry clothes and blankets were provided, and everyone needing medical attention was taken care of by the ship's doctor.

But their ordeal was not over. On reaching Greenock next morning, the internees were put ashore in three groups, Germans, Italians, and sick people. The Italians and Germans were marched off. The sick remained on the quay for full two hours without shelter, and had to march then to a first-aid station, where they had to wait another two and a half hours before ambulances arrived to take them to Mearnskirk Hospital in Newton Mearns.

No preparations had been made for the accommodation of the other group of survivors, who were marched off from the quay, most of them barefoot, to a factory building half a mile distant. No blankets were available, and the only food issued that day was a slice of bread with corned beef and a cup of tea. No water was given for washing until late in the evening of the next day; lavatory accommodation was two water closets for two hundred and fifty men; there were no beds or palliasses and hardly any blankets. All in great need of a hot shower, a good night's rest, and some proper hot food as well as warm clothes, they had to endure another night and day of exposure in their torn and oily clothes. As a result of this, a number of internees became so exhausted that they, too, had to be taken to hospital.

Of the eight hundred and five people who lost their lives on the *Arandora Star*, four hundred and eighty six were Italians. This disaster led to vigorous protests about the British internment policy, which was changed to internment of enemy aliens in camps in Britain only. Most internees had been released by the end of 1942. Of those that remained, many were repatriated from 1943 onwards. It was not, however, until late 1945 that the last internees were finally released.

The butter ration was cut from six to four ounces, and Purchase Tax, the forerunner of VAT, was introduced.

Traders accepted war as a challenge. Advertisements said that war or no war, you must be smart. Wrigleys chewing gum makers claimed that in times of stress, chewing quietened your nerves. An estate agent began a campaign on house buying against Hitler.

'When by self imposed thrift one and a half million British citizens put their small and hard earned savings into homes, they acquire a stake in the country for which they will fight and fight dearly.'

Later, many of those citizens would see their stake reduced to dust and rubble. Iron railings providing no essential purpose had to be removed. A Spitfire Fund was begun with four hundred pounds donated the first week, but it was criticised by those who felt the money would be better earmarked for those who might be rendered homeless.

From the beginning of the war, the civil defence organisations relied heavily on voluntary effort. More policemen were needed, but the regular force wasn't allowed to recruit new members and the War Reserve Recruits were not coming in fast enough.

In 1939 the Woman's Auxiliary Police Corps or WAPC had been formed, but its members were employed only in miscellaneous duties, as drivers, clerkesses, telephonists and typists. It was not till 1943, that five women were appointed to the WAPC in Fife. During the war, because Methil was a port for both naval and merchant ships, the problem of prostitution, and the need for female officers to deal with it, was very much under consideration, but the general feeling in the force was that women officers were unnecessary.

In 1944, the Inspector at Methil submitted a report to the Scottish Home Department, in St Andrews House saying that there were a number of loose immoral women in Methil but they were afraid of being caught by the police and, during the summer months, some of them would take a bus out of the town, and out of the reach and sight of the Police. During the dark nights, they did their trade nearer home but though he had searched for these women, it was a very difficult job for men in uniform to follow and detect women and men 'when they are on such a purpose.'

He claimed that most evidence was hearsay only. Some women in Methil always attended the public houses, but numbers had increased since the war started. A large number of men and women from England had come to the town and, as it is a custom in England for men and their wives to frequent public houses, this custom had crept into the women folks here. It was now a common sight to see a local man and his wife visiting the public houses in Methil and having a drink together.

One woman explained to the Inspector that her doctor had advised her to take a drop of gin. She couldn't afford to buy a bottle, so had to go to the pub. He then went on to say that the doctor verified her statement. He believed that music and singing in public houses were partly the cause of the most of the women frequenting them and, while there, they met all classes of humanity.

Local doctors denied the prevalence of venereal disease among the seamen and women in Methil, with only one local case in the last two months. Several men on board the ships in convoy had contracted the disease at the other ports.

But though there were few charges of prostitution over the years, a number of women were charged, and occasionally sent to prison, for failing to report the presence of an alien. They had in fact taken foreign sailors into their own homes, and because the whereabouts of aliens should be known to the police at all times, they were breaking the law by inviting them in. One of the excuses given was that the woman had asked the sailor home to prevent him falling into the harbour and getting drowned.

Of more interest to the law abiding community, men of thirty five had to register for call up and it was expected the age would go up to forty one. The Department of Health took over local halls to accommodate people bombed out of their homes, and issued guidelines to householders. Up to forty thousand men were now reported to be in German prisoner of war camps, but the good news was that some of those were men who had earlier been reported missing.

For children, plans for compulsory immunisation against diphtheria were being finalised. The disease was increasing in virulence and in numbers, and the aim was to vaccinate at least seventy five per cent of school and pre-school children. The scheme was carried out successfully and at least eighty percent of all children in the area were immunised.

SS Arandora Star

CHAPTER THREE - 1941

With the amount of knowledge we have now, it is difficult to understand just how little people knew about events beyond their immediate locality in the war years. They were dependent on newspapers and the radio for information, and from 1941 onwards, a security blackout was in force. A new sense of seriousness is evident. There are no more stories of adventures and miraculous escapes, just increasing notices of men killed in action or in prisoner of war camps.

One of the first casualties of the year was Billy Fullerton, one of the original members of Fife Flyers. An RAF pilot, he had been in the volunteer reserve squadron, and was called up on the outbreak of war. The enormous scale of the prisoner of war problem is illustrated by the numbers of Red Cross parcels packed each week. Six thousand parcels per week were required to ensure each prisoner received some comforts from home, and Scottish branches offered to help because of English difficulties with bombing raids. The British Red Cross was not allowed to deliver parcels, this was done by the International Red Cross, and after the surrender of France, there was no postal communication with the continent for a long time.

Recruiting was stepped up. A WAAF recruiting officer visited Fife, asking for women between eighteen and forty three to join. Administration staff were also wanted, with an upper age limit of fifty for women who had been in the first war.

More women were wanted for war work, and governments checks were to be made to ascertain what jobs could be done by women. A new Air Training Cadet scheme was to prepare boys between sixteen and eighteen for service in the air. Men under eighteen and over thirty six were to register.

The fear of incendiary bombing was uppermost in people's minds, fire fighting parties were set up, and a deputation from Buckhaven, Methil and Leven Town Councils went to

Liverpool to gain experience of what to do when a town was blitzed.

Sandbags were delivered to every house and stirrup pumps sold at a pound each, but there were bigger dangers than the threat of fire bombs, and this danger was already on the doorstep. Because of the blackout, Methil docks was an extremely dangerous place. James Storrar of Methil, a coal trimmer drowned when he fell into the water. Three seamen and another coal trimmer had also fallen into the dock in the space of a week. The growing death rate was a matter of concern and LNER were asked to provide a system of low powered shaded lights.

Because of security, place names were not mentioned but the Ministry of Home Security warned about exploding mines, and the dangers of any suspicious looking container. Somewhere in Scotland, some boys were killed by an explosion when trying to unscrew a part of an unexploded shell. On February 5th, the Leven Mail published a Ministry of Home Security report that 'Inhabitants of a Scottish town saw a mine floating near the shore. They pulled it in, it exploded, killing three men and injuring two.'

Because of the secrecy surrounding the incident, it is only recently that details have been revealed. On January 23rd, 1941, a mine exploded near Lady's Rock in West Wemyss, killing fifteen year old Peter Graham and four miners. In Buckhaven another mine disaster resulted in the death of ten people, eight of them children.

There were probably many similar accidents around the country but outside their own immediate area, they would not have been publicised, and were allowed to slip out of public memory of everyone except those immediately involved.

One of the most unusual incidents of the war took place in May 1941. Rudolf Hess, deputy leader of the Nazi Party, long-standing confidant of Adolf Hitler and Chairman of the Central Political Commission of the Nazi Party, parachuted from a Messerschmidt-110, after an extraordinary solo, five hour, nine hundred mile flight into Scotland on a 'peace mission' just before the Nazi invasion of the Soviet Union. It was an attempt to make contact with the Duke of Hamilton, a friend from a meeting at the pre-war Olympics.

Hess appeared to believe that there was an anti-Churchill, anti-Communist caucus in Great Britain which would work with Germany, but his mission was quickly disowned by the German hierarchy.

Hess's British captors believed him to be mentally unstable and he was ordered to be imprisoned for the duration of the war. After standing trial at Nuremberg as a war criminal, Hess was sentenced to life imprisonment, and committed suicide in 1987 at the age of ninety two.

Shortly after Hess's landing, a secret memorandum from the Scottish Home Department in Edinburgh was sent to Fife's Chief Constable, warning that no airman operating over foreign territory would carry an identity card, and that any parachutist, whether alien or British should be detained in the custody of the police.

Members of the RAF were instructed to report at once to the nearest police station and to establish their identity by making contact with their unit or nearest RAF Establishment. They would be detained till this contact was made and their credentials verified. In view of the measures already in operation to deal with enemy parachutists, there was a possibility that RAF or Allied airmen might be attacked or not receive immediate attention if they were injured, so guidelines were produced.

Parachutists could be divided into two classes, those in distress or armed invaders intent on destruction. The first would be seen escaping from a plane that probably would crash in the area. Some planes now carried a crew of eight, so up to eight men coming down together did not necessarily mean they were enemies.

Any more than that were to be regarded as such. Airmen landing in distress or crews of crashed air craft might include British, Allied or enemy personnel but it was stressed that immediate first aid was to be given if necessary in every case.

Also in May, German troops invaded the British-held island of Crete and ten days later, British forces surrendered. About eighteen thousand Allied troops were rescued from the beaches, but almost as many were taken prisoner, and the cruiser HMS *Calcutta* was sunk while assisting the evacuation.

Of greater significance to local people was the sinking of the British Royal Navy battle cruiser HMS *Hood*. The Mighty Hood, as she was known, the most famous of all battleships was sunk on 24th May by the German battleship *Bismarck*. By May 1941, submarines destroyed approximately three million tons of Allied shipping. Naval vessels had accounted for one hundred and sixteen tons in January alone.

Hood was built in 1920, but was still fast for her size with deadly guns but an outdated gunnery system. *Bismarck*, one of the best ships of her time was launched in 1939, with state of the art electronics and rapid firing gunnery systems. After commissioning she proceeded to the Arctic and from there planned to break out into the Atlantic via the Denmark Strait, Once in the Atlantic she would have posed an enormous threat to Allied shipping. .

Hood left Scapa Flow early on May 22nd to find and destroy her, but in the battle that followed Hood herself was destroyed. Shells hit her ammunition lockers, setting off rocket mines; more hits, five in all, caused a devastating series of massive explosions. *Hood* rolled to port and went down stern first. Only three men survived out of a crew of one thousand four hundred and eighteen. They made their way to small three foot square rafts floating in the wreckage. Soaked, caked with oil and in a state of shock, they were soon suffering from hypothermia, but were picked up and taken to Rekjavik on May 24th.

Three days later the *Bismarck* was hunted down and destroyed, with only one hundred and fifteen survivors out of a crew of over two thousand. All but five of these survivors were picked up by British ships, but they were forced to give up rescue attempts because of the fear of U-boat attacks.

Though Fife had little experience of bombing, there was always an awareness that it might be their turn next. People had stood and watched the planes going over night after night to bomb Clydeside, the home of the great shipbuilding yards which produced battleships like *Hood, Dreadnought* and *Invincible* and the liners *Lusitania and Aquitania* .

For two nights in March, over two hundred bombers took off from their bases in France, Holland, Denmark and Germany and attacked Clydebank and the Govan shipyards, dropping over a hundred thousand incendiary bombs. Among the buildings damaged was a distillery and a timber yard. The blaze from the raid lit up the sky and could be seen more than twenty five miles away. In all, over five hundred were killed, over six hundred injured and thousands of homes destroyed.

In May, German bombers assaulted London in what was to be the final heavy mission of the Battle of Britain. More than five hundred aircraft dropped high-explosive and incendiary bombs which caused more than three thousand casualties, but the Battle of Britain had been lost, and with it had gone Germany's chance of winning the war.

Johnstone Gillespie Patrick, a Methil man wrote a letter from London, describing conditions there:

'For nearly seven months, day and night, this great city has been subjected to one continuous air battle..... The Germans have claimed that over two thousand tons of bombs were dropped in the first fortnight... This last weeks' raids have hit the poorest most – homes ruined, savings gone, churches and hospitals damaged and many large businesses destroyed.'

Fear of bombing, however, was gradually replaced by fear of invasion with newspapers providing a list of handy hints, for example: 'Don't tell the enemy anything, don't help him in any way. In areas away from fighting, carry on as normal, send your children to school. If you receive the order to 'Stand Firm,' stay indoors or in shelters. At work, carry on as long as possible but take cover when danger approaches. If you see tanks, don't assume that the enemy are in control. There will be times when you have to take orders from the military but with a bit of common sense you can tell if a soldier is really British. Church bells will warn that troops have landed in that neighbourhood.'

With the hindsight of sixty years, it is easy to dismiss this and following warnings as a kind of bungling Dad's Army bureaucracy, but Hitler's forces were rampaging through Europe. Poland, Belgium, The Netherlands and France were all under Nazi rule, and the threat of invasion was very real.

Fife decided to hold a War Weapons Week of fund raising, concerts, events and exhibitions. Lord Elgin was hoping to get the plane in which Hess flew to Scotland as the centre point of an exhibition, but he was unsuccessful. A London Weapons Week had raised over a million pounds and Fife hoped to raise at least a quarter of that. In fact, Leven raised £125,000 in two days.

Living conditions were grim. The butter ration was halved to two ounces a week and eggs had to be sold to the Ministry of Food. A *Grow Food and Save Ships* campaign began. If people became self sufficient the need for merchant vessels would be reduced. Only ten allotments were in use in the Leven area and the Wemyss Coal Company made land available for allotments for all their workers. People were told that there was no such thing as food snobbishness in these days, and because tripe was unrationed it was now being used in the best circles. A recipe for 'tripe olives' was given which involved slices of potato being rolled in pieces of tripe. Before long, corned beef would form a staple of the British diet as a part of the meat ration.

Miners were urged to work a six day week and produce an extra seven thousand tons of coal per week. They were expected to earn their extra cheese ration, and they did, producing an extra eight thousand tons, but a farcical situation arose. Because of lack of fuel, one school had to close and supplies at other schools were running dangerously low.

Farm workers were unhappy. In a reserved occupation, earning fifty five shillings a week, they watched unskilled labourers working on aerodrome building and earning almost double that. Some, at least, would have been probably quite happy to learn that agricultural workers were to be called up, and several thousand conscientious objectors were already employed on the land.

There was good news for one Leven family when their son, Andrew Boyter, missing since the battle of Crete, arrived home unannounced after a journey of almost nineteen thousand miles. Andrew's father had heard a radio report that his ship had been hit by three bombs and when they heard no word, assumed the worst, but Andrew was picked up by another ship. He eventually found himself in Alexandria and after a circuitous journey by the Cape and South America, he reached Halifax in Canada before getting home.

By the second anniversary of the war starting, the manpower shortage in the forces was severe, so reserved occupations for women were cut. Women couldn't be conscripted into the services, according to report, but would have to do industrial work if they didn't join up. Everyone, apart from women with children under the age of fourteen, would be given the choice of volunteering for the forces, Civil Defence, Nursing, Land Army or NAAFI, or be directed into various branches of munitions. People were asked to lend their savings to build warships.

As well as problems of food shortages and rationing to be coped with, there were the pettifogging bureaucrats who seemed to spend an inordinate time in framing hundreds of new rules. A Fife butcher was charged under the Sausages (Maximum Price Order) 1941, for failing to provide a description of the meat they contained, and the Food Ministry banned the slicing and wrapping of bread. Part of the weekly meat ration had to be taken in corn beef.

Food shop assistants were no longer to be exempt from service and all those between twenty and twenty five had to register. Lamp posts, railing and iron gates had to be removed and sent for salvage, and the number of bus stops reduced. You could be fined for wasting paper, or even for taking photographs near the docks, and thirty seven campers who spent their vacation in huts they owned or rented at Burntisland were charged under the Camping Restriction Order. This forbade camping within ten miles of the high water mark anywhere on the east coast of Britain.

In spite of hardships, the Buckhaven and Methil Anglo-Soviet Unity Committee raised five hundred pounds to buy an ambulance to be sent to the Soviet people, who were suffering almost unbelievable hardship which would get worse as winter approached.

One of the few war reports came from the captain of the SS *Rudmore*. Captain E.H. Thomson from Buckhaven brought down a German raider attacker which had tried to bomb him. He believed that the *Rudmore* was the most bombed ship in Britain and was the first British Merchant ship to be attacked in the war.

By the end of the year, the war had entered a new phase. In July, the American President Franklin D. Roosevelt ordered that all Japanese assets should be frozen, all trade with Japan suspended and an embargo laid on oil. On 7th December, Japanese aircraft launched a surprise attack on American naval forces at Pearl Harbour, Hawaii, and the Imperial Government of Japan declared war on Britain. Next day the United States declared war on Japan, and Winston Churchill informed the British parliament that Britain now had to fight on another front.

On the 10th, Japanese aircraft sank the British Royal Navy ships *Prince of Wales* and *Repulse* off the coast of Malaya, and Japanese troops landed at Luzon in The Philippines. On the 11th, Germany and Italy declared war on the United States and signed a new military alliance with Japan, and on Christmas Day, British forces surrendered Hong Kong to the Japanese.

CHAPTER FOUR - 1942

1942 began with boys of seventeen having to register for call up and the possibility of sixteen year olds also being registered. Fear of invasion was still rife. Provost Nairn published a letter to the Burgh of Leven telling them what to do in the event of enemy troops landing. Despite what people might have heard regarding atrocities committed by invading armies, he said, they were to carry on as normal.

'Offer no resistance, do not endeavour to secure and use in defence lethal weapons such as spikes, scythes, forks etc. Read the leaflet *Beating The Invader* and carry out the instructions therein.'

If fires were started, people were to do their best to beat out the conflagration but to take care not to get shot. There was a belief that secret invasion committees had been set up in some parts of the country, and one letter to the Mail outlined the absurdities of the situation exposed by the Provost's letter. *Beating The Invader,* it said, was already out of date. Did the Government intend to wait till the invasion begins before issuing directions about food supplies and so on?

Another letter in the same issue, February 18th, claimed that supplies of food were stored in excellent depots conveniently situated for distribution of supplies when the time comes. 'It will,' he says, 'be iron rations packed in tins and is to be kept unopened till you have finished all other supplies and are forced to use it. Some foods have been packed into containers for six to eight people so you will have to form yourselves into groups of eight, sixteen or twenty four then decide who will take charge of the containers.'

The letter ends by saying 'Once you have got the food, do all you can to keep it in a safe condition. Hide it. Keep it as a last reserve. Do not let it fall into enemy hands.'

It is probably as well that the government and local organisations were never called on to put their invasion plans into action, but at the time any order would have been accepted almost without question.

Another letter to the press spelled out the danger that Britain was in. 'We have been at war for approximately two years, been brushed out at Dunkirk, Norway, Greece and Crete, driven back from Benghazi, swept like an old dust heap in the east by the Japs and probably by the time this is in print, will have lost the Malay peninsula including Singapore.....'

In fact, Singapore was surrendered to the Japanese army on February 15th, with British losses of nearly a hundred and forty thousand men .

Speakers at Rotary and other club meetings provided graphic accounts of what defeat would mean. With pictures taken in occupied countries, they showed how Hitler had brought to Poland conditions comparable to the darkest Middle Ages, and how Holland had been invaded in May 1940 with thousands of planes and more than fifteen thousand paratroops. They discussed the possibility that rumours of a German attack on Russia might be a cover up for one on this country.

At the same time, there was a small matter of rejoicing with the opening of the new Innerleven Church.

A Fife Warship Week was held with torpedoes, guns and telescopes, and a splinter ridden funnel from *HMS* Cossack on display. Over three million pounds was raised and the money was to go to a new ship to replace the *Dunedin*, which was lost in the Far East. The *Dunedin* was later credited with a most important coup. The tanker *Lothringen* was captured and taken to Bermuda, cutting off vital oil supplies for U-boats, but important Enigma material was found where it had fallen behind a filing cabinet in the wireless room. *Dunedin* was torpedoed in November 1941, and the submarine that wrecked her surfaced and circled but didn't pick up any of the survivors. Half of the ship's crew of about five hundred managed to get on to Carley floats, but were adrift for seventy eight hours and only sixty seven men survived.

In May 1942, invasion committees were set up, probably to settle the unrest caused by the lack of information about invasion plans, but committees had a consultative role only. Their task was to collect knowledge of local conditions, produce a list of places where supplies of picks and shovels, wheelbarrows etc could be obtained; to make lists of all people trained in First Aid and find alternate sources of drinking water.

In July, after an eight month siege, in which they dropped almost twenty thousand tons of bombs, nearly as much as the total dropped on the UK during 1941, German and Romanian troops captured Sevastopol, in Russia. On 19th August, an unsuccessful British raid on Dieppe in August by British and Canadian commandos, with tanks and air support, ended with the defeat and capture of the commandos. The Battle of Stalingrad began in September.

Fife's medical officer, Dr GM Fyfe, made a reassuring statement about the possibility of an outbreak of smallpox. Fears had been expressed because the disease had appeared in Glasgow and there were a number of Glasgow people in the area. There had been, he said, one case which broke out in another part of Fife and had been removed from the area. The danger of cases emanating from that one had now passed. His confidence was short lived however. On October 14th, The Leven Mail announced an out break of smallpox in Methilhill. Of the five families affected, ten people had been admitted to hospital, and two of these, thirty four year old Mrs Mackie and her four year old daughter, had died.

The illness was first thought to be chickenpox and the Department of Health issued a warning to all doctors to thoroughly examine any doubtful cases and report them to the local Medical Officer of Health.

The outbreak gave rise to a crop of rumours as to its origin and a popular belief that it originated from a ship in Methil Docks was denied. A visitor from Glasgow was a possible contender because of a recent outbreak there, but it was impossible to establish this. A programme of vaccination was put into force immediately and within a few days, over eighteen thousand people in the Methilhill, Buckhaven,

Denbeath, Methil and Leven area had been vaccinated. Local doctors and health officers were helped by volunteers from medical students, Civil Defence, First Aid personnel and Civil Nursing Reserves. The WVS and Wardens assisted by preparing bandages, giving guidance and disseminating information about the various vaccination centres. Wardens made door-to-door calls asking people if they had been vaccinated and strongly advising them to have it done.

A thorough investigation into all possible contacts with patients was made and, when identified, they were kept under daily observation. It was emphasised that people affected were not infectious till the rash appeared and other symptoms would appear before then, when the contact would be immediately quarantined.

The following week, the paper reported that another eighteen people were in hospital suffering from smallpox, all of them contacts of the first lot of patients. One of these was from Milton of Balgonie, and was a direct contact from the Methilhill outbreak. The third victim was a young woman, Janet Donald, who resided with her parents at 1 Kirk Park, Methilhill. There were now twenty five cases in hospital, including boys aged fourteen and seven and girls of fourteen, twelve and eight.

The news that the period Thursday to Monday had added eighteen cases to the list, and that a third death had occurred, created renewed concern in the public mind. All the cases were according to the medical authorities, under close observation, and were contacts of previous cases. On Monday a case was reported from Larkhall in Lanarkshire, where a woman was detained for observation. It was announced that the woman had visited relatives at Methilhill, and had probably become a contact.

On Monday night, Dr Fyfe urged in an appeal broadcast that all persons who had known themselves to be contacts should immediately inform the authorities. It was not helpful to conceal any information that would help towards limiting the spread of infection.

Levenmouth at War

In a statement at the weekend Dr Fyfe said that the eight surviving cases of the original ten were getting on exceptionally well. All the later cases were direct contacts of previous cases and had been under observation and symptoms detected at an early stage.

All of them were vaccinated but only after they had become infected. Nevertheless the fact that they had been vaccinated before the disease developed would stand them in very good stead. Their condition was very much milder that the first cases. Dr Fyfe also commented on the remarkable vaccination record achieved in the affected area. Out of a population of thirty one thousand, over eighty per cent had been vaccinated in a week, twenty thousand at the public clinics and six thousand by private practitioners.

Dr Fyffe said that the Department of Health had expressed amazement at the exceptional percentage of people who responded to the call for vaccination. "I have no comparative figures, but I believe it must be the largest number of people vaccinated in any area in so short a time. There is no doubt that the people have responded magnificently and I think we can now say we have thrown up a safety curtain between the public and the risk of infection spreading."

The death toll rose to five with the announcement of another two fatalities, twenty three year old John Torrance and Mrs Gourlay aged twenty one, both of Pirnie Street, Methilhill.

These two deaths had a very tragic bearing on one Methilhill family. Mrs Gourlay and Mr Torrance were the daughter and son of Mr and Mrs Torrance, Simon Crescent. Mrs Mackie, whose death with that of her four year old daughter, was reported the week before, was also a daughter of Mr and Mrs Torrance, so that in one week, the family lost two daughters, a son and a grandchild.

By the end of the month, Mrs Helen Simpson and her daughter Mrs Walton, both of Pirnie Street, Methilhill had brought the toll to seven. The only note of hope was that no new cases had been reported since October 18th.

The powers that be were praying for the third of November, which would be the 'clear date' and would signify the end of the outbreak. The Public Heath Committee discussed the problems raised by the epidemic. Throughout the progress of the disease, considerable fear was generated by the way contacts were dealt with, and grave disquiet felt about the way 'they were allowed to wander about.'

The Medical Officer had instructed all the one hundred and fifteen contacts to stay away from work and school and not to mix with the general public, but while some families co-operated, others didn't. Miners who had been in contact with cases, but persisted in going to work, almost caused a strike at the Michael Colliery, and the intervention of the Sanitary Inspector was required to pacify the situation. It was all very well for public health officials to say that contacts had a moral obligation to their fellow men, but because men were able bodied, they could be refused Public Assistance.

Families of those in hospital were still living in their homes, but the authorities had no powers to move them out and no place to put them if they had. Besides, such a move was not strictly necessary; the measures put in place had succeeded in checking the progress of the disease. They had built up 'a wall of vaccination' round the area. The ration books, belonging to those affected and their contacts, had been collected and destroyed. New cards would be issued directly to the shops.

However, a decision was made to authorise the setting up of a reception house for direct contacts should it become necessary. People should be told that there were penalties that could be imposed if they did not conform to the Public Health Act, or if their actions encouraged the spread of infection. Mr J McArthur, of Buckhaven was worried about the effects of the disease extending to other areas.

'If this spreads to West Fife, you will lose half of West Fife's coal output for at least a week through the effects of mass vaccination... if we can stop this, we are doing a valuable national service.'

Levenmouth at War

Vaccination, he said was a serious business. A number of miners and bus conductresses were off work as a result and there was a tremendous loss of output to the nation. There was a general feeling of alarm, and an isolation home for up to fifty people would be cheap and would give the public confidence. A question was later asked in Parliament about the outbreak and it was claimed that only nine people in Scotland had died from smallpox. The cause of death for other reported victims was not smallpox. One of the difficulties was in diagnosis because of the similarity with chickenpox in the early stages of the disease, and a lack of experience on the part of medical officers in dealing with smallpox.

Fife's own battleship HMS Bellona

Meanwhile, another war, not against disease, was being fought. In November there was the news that Leading Wireman James Thomson Nesbit, from Methil, had received the Distinguished Service Medal from the King at Buckingham Palace. James had gone overboard in wintry seas when the ship's minesweeping gear had been knocked out of

order by some obstruction. The captain called for two
volunteers and Nesbit and a colleague went overboard in
darkness and heavy seas with ropes lashed round their bodies.
In spite of icy cold waves they got themselves into an
awkward and dangerous position to free the gear.

Other stories did not have such a happy ending. In
December, six Methil seamen were lost – Alexander Herd,
from Buckhaven; George Jackson, William Marshall, John
Smith, William Marshall, William Watson and John Suttie
from Methil. Watson had already survived being torpedoed in
the second month of the war. His brother was one of only four
survivors rescued after clinging to a raft for seven hours in
wintry seas. Suttie had been going to sea since the age of
fifteen. At the evacuation of Norway, while his ship was lying
off a Norwegian port, a Nazi flag appeared hanging over a
wall. The Captain offered a bet that no-one was brave enough
to go ashore and capture it. Suttie won the bet and brought the
flag home as a souvenir.

Many sailors had reason to bless Methil's Flying Angel
Mission. At the beginning of the war, the arches at the docks
were desolate and disused, but a transformation had taken
place. Eight hundred pounds were raised in Fife to provide
accommodation for visiting seamen and shipwrecked sailors.
It was run with the help of local volunteers and shortly after it
opened, the warden Mr Price paid tribute to the merchant
seamen.

'These men don't have the privilege of wearing a uniform
or wearing a badge to show which regiment they belong to.
They just go on with their everyday work. Time after time, I
meet men who have been torpedoed one, two, three, even four
times and they always turn up at the port to go on with their
every day work.'

In September 1942, an extension was built to provide
facilities for Master Mariners and Officers as well as other
ranks. Support came from all over Scotland, but principally
from Fife, and the extension was opened by Lady Victoria
Wemyss. A handsome memorial Bible was dedicated to the

Mission as a gift from sisters from Leven. The dedication read:

A gift to the Flying Angel Seamen's Mission in recognition of its valuable work and in proud and loving remembrance of Alexander Bissett, Lt. RN, aged 27 years and his many brave comrades who gave their lives for their country in His Majesty's Ship Barham in November 1941.

The *Barham* formed part of the Home Fleet in 1939, was involved in operations in the Mediterranean, supported ships at the Battle of the Nile, and took part in the battle for Crete. She was hit several times and was finally torpedoed by a German submarine. As she rolled over to port, her after magazines exploded and she sank very quickly. Over two thirds of her crew were lost.

The *Barham* featured in one of the most unusual episodes of the war. Helen Duncan, born in Callander in 1897, was a middle–aged mother of six when, in 1944, she became the last person in Britain to be tried under the 1735 Witchcraft Act. She was an acclaimed medium, giving séances all over the country and at her trial over forty witnesses appeared on her behalf.

A materialistic medium, it is believed in some quarters that Mrs Duncan was the victim of a government conspiracy to keep her silent. She was deemed a security risk after a dead sailor 'appeared' at a séance she held in Portsmouth, and told the people there that his ship had gone down. The sinking of his battleship, *HMS Barham,* off the coast of Malta in 1941, had been kept secret by the War Office for some time. No action was taken against Duncan, however, till three years later when she was arrested and charged with pretending to conjure up the spirits of the dead . The prosecution claimed she was a fraud, cashing in on vulnerable families who had lost loved ones, and she was sent to prison for nine months.

In 1997, a campaign was launched to clear her name and gain a posthumous pardon. Why did it take three years to bring her to court, and why was her trial held in London instead of Portsmouth where the 'crime' was committed?

Supporters believe that the Government were afraid that she might leak information on the proposed D-day landings in Normandy. Three years after her death, according to an article in *The Scotsman*, Scotland's head of intelligence wrote that she was a dangerous person and that her information was authentic. Whatever opinions there might be, and she had as many famous supporters as detractors, one thing is clear. She did tell a mother that her son had been lost on the *Barham*, which the authorities had failed to do.

HMS Barham

CHAPTER FIVE - 1943

1943 provided a turning point, when people began to believe that the war could be won. A series of raids on the Ruhr was begun and a four day air attack was launched on a Japanese convoy off New Guinea. Russian leaders demanded the surrender of the German 6th Army, after bitter fighting during the battle of Stalingrad.

The Methil Anglo–Soviet Unity Committee raised nearly three thousand pounds for the Aid to Russia Fund, and a mobile X-ray unit was bought. The Provost said that our allies still had to bear the brunt of the battle and ended by saying, 'We extend our admiration to them and their great leader Stalin.'

Gunner A.R. Smith of Leven was mentioned in dispatches when he rescued from drowning, a car driver whose car had backed into a tank of water ten to twelve feet deep. The driver tried to open the door, which was the wrong thing to do because it would have sunk immediately. Smith plunged in, wearing boots, puttees and webbing equipment and dragged the man out. Smith had worked at the National Steel Foundry before joining up and was a well known member of Leven Swimming Club.

Thirty one year old Squadron Leader Bruce Morton DFC, from Leven, described his bout with Nazi fighters. He brought his plane home with gun turrets and instruments out of action, rudder jammed, petrol tanks holed, and wireless operator and navigator both wounded. He had been awarded his DFC in a previous incident in 1942, when he was wounded in the knee and spent several weeks in hospital.

At home, problems were much simpler to deal with. Coal merchants were fined for supplying non-registered customers, and maximum prices were fixed for green vegetables. Shop keepers were banned from selling tinned vegetables because fresh ones were available. Two people in St Andrews died from eating sausages with arsenic in them. Utility furniture was introduced and it was illegal to make any other kind.

Vandalism is not a twenty first century occupation. Shelters were damaged and filled with rubbish and old furniture, and nearly a thousand windows were broken in one weekend at a railway yard. A twenty year old youth was charged with housebreaking and stealing a bicycle. The sheriff said that 'What I'd like to do with some of you young boys is to order a good thrashing, the most proper thrashing of your life. But I cannot do it. We are not allowed to thrash you little darlings.'

It wasn't only youth who were being threatened with the law. It came to the notice of the authorities that the gates and railings which had been removed for salvage were being replaced 'promiscuously' by wooden gates and fences. Guidance was sought from the Ministry of Works, who insisted that the new wooden railings were contrary to regulations. Joiners carrying out such work would be transferred to National Service work.

Voluntary staff at the library went on strike because paid assistants were to be employed so that the library could open for longer. Volunteers locked the door and even members of the Library Committee were unable to gain access. Paid assistants, the volunteers claimed, were quite unnecessary and the money would be better spent on buying books, and they eventually 'severed all connections with the library.'

Gleneagles, taken over at the start of the war as an emergency hospital, was turned into a fitness centre, with room for two hundred disabled miners. It was necessary to get injured men back to work as quickly as possible. Those who could work but wouldn't were fined or sent to prison for absenteeism, and at a shareholders meeting Augustus Carlow, Chairman of the Fife Coal Company outlined plans for a new colliery, The Michael, which was opened later in the year by Willie Gallacher, MP for West Fife..

The Flying Angel celebrated another year, in which a hundred and forty thousand men had visited the Mission. Eight hundred were entertained at Christmas and social activities included taking men to football matches, boxing, bowling and golf.

In April, the first prisoners to be repatriated after a raid on the Italian base of Spezia arrived home, after travelling through France, Spain and Portugal. In Spain, people gave them food they could ill spare. Lance Corporal John Drylie Wishart was awarded the Military Medal for rescuing wounded colleagues and bringing them through enemy lines in the Western desert. He saved two Black Watch men, tended their wounds and brought them in despite heavy shelling.

May saw the end of the war in North Africa. Bizerta and Tunis were captured by the Allies, and over two hundred thousand German and Italian prisoners of war were taken. After the British victory at the battle of El Alamein in November 1942, General Rommel's army had retreated across North Africa to Tunisia. This new attempt at fresh offensives failed and General Montgomery broke through his positions in early April 1943. Forced to retreat again, Rommel's forces were deprived of food and supplies by the Allies. They surrendered on 13th May.

The Opera House Algiers – green trams were for Europeans, brown trams for Arab underclass

Three days after the surrender, the R.A.F destroyed the Möhnesee and Eider Dams.

Also celebrated, on the instructions of Winston Churchill , was the third anniversary of the Home Guard. Fife's 4th Battallion from Wemyss, Buckhaven, Methil, Methilhill, Leven, Kennoway and Windygates paraded, gave a display and demonstration of weapons, and attended a service, accompanied by the Wellesley Colliery Band. The day ended with a film show. A school for training rescue brigades in tunnelling opened in Methil and a Wings for Victory Week included exhibitions, boxing tournaments and concerts.

Glencoe MacDonald, a twenty one year old merchant seaman was awarded the MBE after his ship was torpedoed. The ship's captain explained that he and five of the crew stayed behind to try and keep the ship afloat. The one hundred and sixty people aboard included ninety passengers. Glen's story is remarkably matter of fact.

'We got them away on rafts and they were all picked up by other ships. The engine room was flooded and the fires were out. The engineers and firemen worked heroically getting pumps working and re-lighting fires. The ship listed to twenty degrees and then forty degrees and with the water gaining on us, we tried to manhandle a big auxiliary pump into the engine room. After a terrific struggle, we had to give up. I scrambled down into the water, and managed to pick up a lifeboat light and clung to it. Then I found a float and got on to it. I was picked up two hours later.'

The Captain, William Thomas Dawson, received an OBE. The men's action was described as displaying great gallantry and skill in saving lives and trying to save their torpedoed vessel in most dangerous circumstances. MacDonald had joined the merchant service with Salveson of Leith, and had been torpedoed on his first voyage.

At a meeting of the Town Council, the Provost and council expressed their pleasure at the award and forwarded congratulations. Corporal William Wilson, from East Wemyss, was one of three Fifers to get the Military Medal.

The twenty four year old had taken part in fighting in the Middle East and was present during the victorious march of the Allied armies through Tripoli.

The Reverend W R Copeland, whose mother lived in Buckhaven, was coming home after two years as a padre in the Middle East when his ship was torpedoed. One of his colleagues explained that the padre was wounded but stayed aboard and helped people into the life boats.

The boats tried to keep together as much as possible, and the U-boat cruised between them, taking off women, children and wounded men. When it moved off, the British were once more transferred to lifeboats. The padre was very weak by this time and must have decided he was becoming a burden, so he slipped from the lifeboat during the transfer.

The Red Cross organised a Prisoner of War Week. Eighty six local men in prison were each sent a ten shilling parcel every week at a local cost of nearly two and a half thousand pounds. Altogether over a thousand pounds were raised, with one boy donating his collection of a hundred and forty five farthings.

The Red Cross asked for occupational parcels for wounded prisoners with tapestry, embroidery, basket work, rug making and so on to occupy their minds. Slippers were popular and waistcoats for embroidering, and also required were working gloves, book binding equipment to preserve and repair books in camp libraries. Spinning, weaving, netting and fly tying were also popular.

Serving soldiers with time on their hands found other ways of filling it. One of the men who produced the first British newspaper in Tunisia, *The Times Telegraph*, was Private Edward Phenix from Buckhaven, who had worked at Allen Litho. The paper was on the street within twenty four hours of the Germans clearing out of the country.

At the same time, the Allied forces invaded Sicily, in one of the greatest airborne-amphibious operations of the war with three thousand ships and landing craft, a hundred and sixty thousand men, plus vehicles, tanks and guns. The Allies then moved on to invade Italy in September and gained their first foothold on the continental mainland since 1940. Unknown at the time, except to a select few, Roosevelt and Churchill met in Quebec to discuss plans for the invasion of Normandy and agreed that Admiral Lord Louis Mountbatten should serve as chief for the new Southeast Asia Command.

At home, there was good news for tea drinkers. Lord Woolton, the Food Minister had managed to buy the whole of the year's crop, over three thousand tons. There would be a distribution of onions later in the month, but soft drinks were in short supply. Woolton recommended whisky drinkers to use water instead of soda as they would soon get used to it.

Returning soldiers had stories of hardship and bravery to tell. Flight Lieutenant William Gallacher, from Methil, who was part of the aircrew taking Churchill and the King on their separate trips to North Africa, was awarded the MVO. The driver of the tank which captured the German General Von Arnhim in the last round up in Tunisia, Lance Corporal Harry Robertson from Methil, told of the General's capture. His tank was part of the 4th India Division, and Von Arnhim surrendered peacefully. Robertson, who had come home as part of a party in charge of prisoners of war, had twice been blown up in a mine field 'getting a bit of a shake' and had seen hundreds of German and Italian soldiers coming in as prisoners without a British Allied escort. His comrade from Methil, trooper Andrew Reid lost his life in Tunisia.

Seventeen year old apprentice John Keddie, who had joined the Merchant Navy at sixteen, was captured in March 1941 and spent three days aboard the *Scharnhorst* and two years in a prison camp in Germany. Keddie's merchant ship was sunk by the *Scharnhorst,* which had figured frequently in early war reports. Survivors were picked up and later transferred to a supply ship which landed them in La Rochelle. They spent ten days in Bordeaux, where French people, who gave them food and cigarettes, also gave the impression that they were desperate for liberation and a chance to evict the German occupiers.

From there they were moved to Bremervord where he was put in 'clink' for three days for refusing to work, but in general their treatment was good. He was taken to Wilhelmshafen for interrogation and survived bombing of the port by the RAF. He felt that recently the Germans had realised they couldn't win. The prisoners organised activities, using sport, musical and theatrical talent. Even the string from the Red Cross parcels was utilised to adorn stage 'beauties.' He paid tribute to the Red Cross, whose parcels provided a link with home.

Keddie, one of a hundred and thirty one troops chosen for repatriation in June, was transferred to another camp where he met a friend, Roger Thomson from Buckhaven, who had been a prisoner since Dieppe. They were taken through Bremen and Cologne then to Lisbon via Brussels, France and Spain. Thanks to the generosity of the Red Cross, they were able to return the kindness of people en route by giving them cigarettes. The men lived in hotels in Lisbon and were given hospitality by the British community.

On arrival home, they were met by members of the Shipwrecked Mariners Association, treated splendidly and given travel vouchers to return home.

Cadet Robert Stuart from Buckhaven, a survivor of the hospital ship Newfoundland which was deliberately bombed and set on fire by German bombers off Salermo, gave a modest account of the incident.

'An aerial torpedo hit us and started a fire. It soon got a hold and the skipper decided to keep on board only a selection of the crew to fight the blaze. Eighteen of us volunteered and we started on the fire while others got away in the boats. It was a longish job but after two days continuous fire fighting, we got the blaze out. All I did was work around with a hose.'

Other Leven and Methilhill returned prisoners were Sergeant David Munro, R.A. Leven, Privates James Kirkpatrick, Black Watch, and Robert Adamson, RAMC. Adamson, who arrived at Leith on the Empress of India, was captured in Belgium in May 1940, marched through France to

Holland, and taken by barge to Dortmund, then to Poland. The first man he met there was Kirkpatrick. Adamson's brother, Thomas, was still in prison. They had been in the same camp for two years, and lots of other Fife men were still in captivity. Kirkpatrick said that without the Red Cross parcels, they would not be there to tell the tale.

He was taken prisoner in May 1940, and with five hundred British comrades and a large body of German troops, spent a week in Tournai, unloading German wounded men from ambulances. Then it was a long trek through Holland where they were kept short of drinking water; a train journey through Germany in cattle trucks, sixty to seventy in each, and on to a camp in Poland. After Kirkpatrick had been there for fourteen weeks, he met a fellow villager from Methil, Private McKinlay. Given eight days detention for insolence, he was forgotten about and was starving when he was released by a RAMC officer.

He spent ten months working in salt mines with Harry Dougall from the Rosie and Bud Maxwell from Denbeath, then eleven months in hospital with salt poisoning. His eyes were badly affected and he was eventually listed for repatriation but instead was sent to a small camp with four hundred Britons. After four weeks, it was on to cattle trucks for Lansdorf where he had to wait a year for his promised repatriation.

While at Lansdorf, he saw Canadian prisoners with their hands tied with string. A British medical officer complained and got handcuffs instead of the string which lacerated the men's wrists. The Germans stopped their Red Cross parcels and offered them to Indian prisoners who refused, saying they were also British troops. On the way home, the men were given a Canadian Red Cross gift of three hundred cigarettes and a British comforts parcel, and were fairly well treated on their train journey to Sweden.

The outstanding memories of both these men was the kindness of the Polish people and the privations suffered by Russian prisoners, who suffered horribly, especially when typhus broke out in 1941-42. It was not unusual to see barefoot thirteen year old Russians working on German railways. The Germans knew they were losing the war and morale was low. They feared the Russians and the punishment for misdemeanours by German soldiers was to be sent to the Russian front.

Sergeant Munro was at Le Panne in Belgium in May 1940. The troops were on the beach and could see the ships waiting to take them off but embarkation was delayed till nightfall. His ankle was badly shattered by a German shell and he was in five different hospitals in Belgium. Later he was taken to Germany, where the food was monotonously poor, potatoes, cabbage and turnip all the time.

Munro was waiting for repatriation when negotiations broke down and the transfer cancelled. He too saw Canadian prisoners with their hands tied. In Lansdorf the doctors managed to save his foot, and he was given one day's notice that he was going home.

'We spent two days crossing Germany, travelling only at night. During the day, we lay up in shunting yards where we could see nothing of the damage inflicted by bombing raids. The Swedish civilians gave us a great welcome, waving torches and calling good luck, and we were given parcels with cigarettes, chocolate, apples and sandwiches. At Gothenburg, we watched the arrival of German prisoners who were being exchanged, but they looked dull and listless compared to the British who were bright and cheery at the prospect of going home.

Black Watch Captain David Richardson had spent two years in a prison camp hospital after being wounded at St Valery. Private James Fairfull was given a special welcome home. He was guest of honour at a function in aid of Church Comforts Fund for service members. Fairfull had done his bit in the first war and his name was inscribed among the fallen on the burgh war memorial. This was described by the Provost as a terminological inexactitude. A social and dance was also held in his honour at the Miners Institute in Denbeath.

Levenmouth at War

Methil man Sergeant T. Braid, RASC, escaped from an Italian prisoner of war camp where he had been since his capture in Tobruk in 1942. With a few companions, he got away just before the Germans took over, and travelled south for hundreds of miles before reaching British lines. They had many scares getting through German lines and met up with a comrade who'd escaped from a train taking him to Germany. Braid said the Germans were taking everything, despoiling Italy of almost anything of any value, including food and clothes.

The Mighty Hood

CHAPTER SIX - 1944

On January 12th, the first Allied attacks on Monte Cassino took place. Cassino, a natural fortress consisting of a town on the slopes of a high mountain crowned by a Benedictine Monastery and skirted to the south by three rivers, formed part of the strongest German defences south of Rome. It had to be captured by the Allies in order to gain access to the Liri Valley, the so-called gateway to Rome. It took till May 18th, often in appalling wet and cold weather with heavy Allied losses, before the Germans evacuated the town, and the monastery was captured by Polish troops. They hoisted their red and white flag on the ruins of Monte Cassino, which the Germans had used as an observation post and artillery position. Two German armies were defeated, twenty thousand prisoners taken, three defence lines smashed, and vast quantities of German material destroyed, but over four thousand Allied troops were killed and four times as many injured.

British bombers dropped two thousand eight hundred tons of bombs on Berlin, and a series of German raids on London and southern England was followed by RAF bombers raids on Berlin, Kiel and Magdeburg. After a siege of two and a half years, Russian troops relieved Leningrad, and British and American forces landed at Anzio and Nettuno in Italy. Captain G. Baird of Methil was to be awarded a DCM for gallantry and devotion to duty at Anzio. Though wounded, he rescued an NCO under fire, and crawled five hundred yards with vital information.

At home, thousands of men aged between eighteen and twenty five were to be called up for work in the mines, and householders were asked to provide board and lodgings for men drafted into the area. When war was declared against Germany in September 1939, the British Government made the mistake of allowing experienced coal miners to be called up into the armed services, either as reservists or as conscripts. Miners were also allowed to transfer into other higher paid industries. It was thought at the time that the gaps in the coal mining industry would be replaced by previously unemployed men and by making the industry a reserved occupation for key workers.

By mid-1943, however, over thirty six thousand coal miners had left the industry for better paid work. The Government decided it needed forty thousand more miners but despite asking service men and conscripts to opt for this reserved occupation, little impact was made on the numbers needed. In December 1943 Ernest Bevin' the wartime Minister of Labour and former leader of the Transport and General Workers Union, masterminded a scheme whereby a ballot took place to put a proportion of conscripted men into the mines instead of the armed services. The only exceptions were men accepted for flying duties in the RAF or Fleet Air Arm, men accepted for work in submarines and men on a shortlist of highly skilled occupations required for armed service trades.

From December 1943 until the end of the war, nearly fifty thousand men were conscripted to work in the coal mines. Named after the Minister, these Bevin Boys represented ten per cent of male conscripts aged between eighteen and twenty five. Mining work was not popular either with the miners or the boys themselves, many of whom had no mining background at all. The cry from mining representatives was. 'Bring back the men you took for the services. For all the good these youths will do in the mines, it won't be much use.'

Later, they were described, unfairly as they had no choice in where they were sent, as being ' a mixed breed, some were escapists, dodgers of low moral character.'

For the young men, there was nothing glamorous or daring about working underground, but refusal would inevitably result in a heavy fine or possible imprisonment under the wartime Emergency Powers Act. Men had the opportunity at the time of call-up of choosing mining in lieu of service in the armed services, and were so classified as Optants or Volunteers. There were suggestions that Bevin Boys were sent to coal mines as conscientious objectors, but there were less than fifty objectors out of nearly fifty thousand Bevin Boys.

Accommodation was in either a purpose built miners hostel similar to an army camp or in billets, at a cost of twenty five shillings a week deducted out of an average wage of three pounds, ten shillings. Training for Bevin Boys serving in Scotland took place at the Government Training Centre Colliery at Muircockhall in Fife, with accommodation at the Miners' Hostel at Townhill.

Training would last for a duration of four weeks and at the end of this period, final allocation would be made to a colliery normally within the region where the training had taken place.

Home Guard exercise at the colliery

Accommodation again would be either in a hostel or private billets. A further two weeks local training was given before starting their mining career. They were equipped with a safety helmet, overalls and steel capped boots, and like other miners carried their safety lamp, a piece tin and a water bottle. Most of the Bevin Boys worked on haulage and conveyor belts with a few graduating to work at the coal face.

Most forms of haulage involved the use of cables for the movement of tubs. In some collieries pit ponies were used for haulage, and they would have to learn to deal with these animals.

Regular miners, most of whom were born and bred in a mining community, relied on bonuses earned by hard work and didn't relish the idea of working alongside unskilled and inexperienced men who didn't want to be there in the first place. The Bevin boys had little or no knowledge of the industry, many of them had never got their hands dirty in their lives, and they were totally unused to manual labour. Miners worked hard in appalling conditions, and accidents and injury were commonplace, as was the fear of explosion resulting in fire or rock fall. Some of the larger collieries were lucky enough to have pit head baths in order to shower and change into clean clothes, others were not so lucky.

Bevin Boys did not have a uniform and therefore only wore civilian clothes when off duty. This could lead to challenges by members of the public as to why they were not in Army, Royal Navy or Royal Air Force uniform. They were suspected of being of either being conscientious objectors, deserters from the forces or a possible enemy. If they became unfit for work underground, they were reassigned to surface work. There was no opportunity to transfer to another industry or the forces. Those Bevin Boys who were injured did not receive a Government pension as they were legally regarded as civilians.

After VE day, a Bevin Boy release scheme was brought into being similar to that of the armed services, but they received no medals or other form of recognition or reward for their services to the war effort in which they played a very vital part. This contrasted with demobilised servicemen who were allowed to keep their uniform, given a demobilisation outfit, paid leave and war and campaign medals. Bevin Boys had no right to return to their pre-war jobs as could demobbed servicemen.

It was not until the 50th Anniversary of the VE and VJ Day Commemorations during May and August of 1995 that Bevin Boys were finally recognised. Speeches made by the Queen, Betty Boothroyd, the Speaker of the House of Commons, and John Major, the Prime Minister at the time, all gave belated honour to the Bevin Boys, and they were finally allowed to take part in the Remembrance Sunday Service held at the Cenotaph, Whitehall. The last of the Bevin Boys were demobbed in 1948 well after the British coal mines were nationalised in 1947. Very few opted to stay on in the mining industry.

But that was still in the future. In January 1944, it was reckoned that another eight thousand miners were needed, and they had to be acquired somehow.

Stories of death, destruction and bravery in war continued to be told. George Low, aged sixteen from Methil, and eighteen year old Michael Brownlie from East Wemyss, arrived home after the sinking of their ship during a raid at Bari in Italy, which cost the allies seventeen ships and over a thousand casualties. Low, who had been in the Merchant Navy for two years, serving as a galley boy said that two of the ships were ammunition ships, which exploded, causing great destruction in the harbour.

'About thirty bombers swept over Bari. They took the defences by surprise and were able to fly very low and pick out their targets. The harbour was crowded so it was impossible for the bombers to miss hitting something. Bombs rained down on the vessels and the bombers also had their machine guns and cannons blazing all the time. It was all over in half an hour but it was a period of terror I'll never forget. As the bombs were falling I took shelter under a gun turret but that was not enough to save me. Ships were being hit all round and ours was one of the last to be struck. Two bombs landed on the deck, aft and amidships. Fire broke out at once and as there was no possibility of fighting it successfully and great danger of our vessel blowing up, orders were given to abandon ship. The third mate was badly wounded but managed to get into a small boat which was rapidly filling up with water. He was helpless, and one man in our boat dived into the water, swam to the boat and rescued him.'

There was an unexpected treat for housewives. Lemons appeared in the shops just in time for Shrove Tuesday, but lemon squeezers were unavailable. They had not been needed for some considerable time. Prohibited was a word that everyone was familiar with then. Every day, it seemed, new regulations, some temporary, others more long lasting, came into force. The sale of marmalade was prohibited but there were hopes of a supply of sardines and tinned peas.

Coastal areas of Fife were placed under a travel ban for six months, and persons not resident in the area were prohibited from entering. The ending of the ban brought relief for Leven's hotels and boarding houses, whose custom had been drastically reduced.

The warship adopted by Fife as a result of their Warship Week, the HMS *Bellona*, came into service. Strict security surrounded her construction so it was not till after the launch that it was known she was built at Govan. *Bellona* was begun in November, 1939, launched in September 1942 and commissioned in October, 1943

Her crest was presented to Fife in October by Admiral Whitworth, Commander in Chief, Rosyth, who gave an account of the ship's history since its commission. *Bellona* had achieved fame in action in the Bay of Biscay.

Bellona's motto was 'Battle is our Business' and she was one of over fifty warships built at the Fairfield ship-building and engineering company's shipyard at Govan on the Clyde. She participated in several Russian Convoys, both before and after D-day. Prior to D-day, she took over Channel patrol in place of HMS *Charybidus*, which had been sunk off the Channel Isles by a radio-controlled bomb. On arrival at Plymouth, *Bellona* was fitted with equipment for jamming the radio signals that controlled the bombs. *Bellona* and seven destroyers were involved in the patrol and their codename was Snow White and the Seven Dwarfs.

During the day, the force anchored in Plymouth Sound, as air defence of Plymouth. At dusk, under cover of darkness and maintaining radio and radar silence, the force would proceed at full speed to the French coast to keep the German Narvik class destroyers bottled up in Brest. *Bellona*'s duty during the D Day landings was to help to support Omaha Beach, the American sector, with the American battleships *Texas* and *Arkansas* .

Information was sometimes given when the government thought it necessary to boost morale. The Ministry of Information published a booklet on the history of the 8th Army from September 1941 to January 1943, ending with an account of the great drive on El Alamein and the leadership of General Montgomery.

Captain Cecil Leon V. Dury from Methil was later in the year at Buckingham Palace to receive a CBE for bravery and distinguished conduct during operations in the Mediterranean. An unusual distinction for the Merchant Navy, it was awarded for bravery and skilful handling of his ship under enemy bombing while engaged in assisting the 8th Army with supplies at Benghazi at a critical moment in the campaign, and for other services of a hazardous nature. Now home after four years, Dury had the most lengthy period of service among Merchant Navy officers in the Mediterranean and had taken part in many salvage operations off the Libyan coast.

In March, Japanese forces invaded India. By May, Pte J. Salmond from Leven was, in India preparing to fight, along with other men of the Black Watch, described as veterans of Crete, Syria, the Middle East and Tobruk.

General Charles de Gaulle became head of the French Provisional Government in London, Gandhi, Indian

Nationalist was released from detention in India, and the German Army's military intelligence unit, the Abwehr, was placed under the control of Heinrich Himmler, the leader of the SS.

On June 6th, Allied forces launched the D-Day invasion of Normandy to free Europe from occupation by German troops. Preparations for this had been going on since the fall of France in 1940, and from 1942 onwards many people believed and hoped that the opening of a 'second front' on the continent would soon be possible. But it was not until the end of 1943 that serious preparations for the re-invasion of Europe across the Channel began. In the south of England seemingly endless convoys of military vehicles and troops of all the Allied nations poured along the roads and railways of Britain towards the sealed coastal area. Much of the training and preparation for D Day took place in Scotland, which had a very important role to play. The Mulberry harbours were made and tested in Scotland. Scottish beaches around the Moray and Dornoch firths were similar to the Normandy beaches, so a huge area was cleared and used a training ground.

At Port Edgar, HMS *Lochinvar* trained mine sweeping crews and, in bases all over Scotland, training in radar, submarine activity, amphibious and other aspects of warfare was given, and supreme efforts were made to keep the operation secret. Part of the deception was the training of a Mountain Division to back up rumours of an invasion of Norway, the quantity of shipping assembled off Methil, and the use of double agents to report on this and other shipping activity. The exact timing and destination of the force had to be kept secret and men did not know until the last possible moment where and when they were going. On 25th August, Paris was liberated by Free French, US, and British forces, and a week later, British forces captured Brussels. Then it was the turn of Holland when Allied paratroops landed in the Netherlands, in the biggest airborne operation ever attempted.

One of the men serving with the liberation army was George Medal winner Lieutenant Allan McDonald from

Buckhaven. He was one of four brothers serving in the armed forces. When an aircraft with its crew and load of bombs crashed near his station, he ignored the danger of bombs exploding, went into the wreckage and pulled two of the crew to safety. He then called for volunteers to help remove unexploded bombs.

Another Fifer, Gunner Thomas Henny from Leven, landed with the airborne troops at Arnhem. He was unwilling to say much about his experiences, but counted himself as one of the lucky ones. Henny helped to bring out a wounded KOSB man and praised the Canadian Royal Engineers who got them across the river, and a movie camera man who kept 'shooting' till the last. Allan Wood, a well-known war correspondent was with Henny during the nine days of the struggle.

By September 1944, the Second World War had almost reached a conclusion. The Allied armies had rapidly pushed the disorganised Germans almost completely out of France and Belgium, and their front line was only a few miles short of the Dutch border. Because of supply problems, the allied armies did not have the resources to keep advancing, and it was agreed that Field Marshal Montgomery and his 2nd British Army would deal the final blow and win the war before the end of 1944.

His plan was to land glider and parachute troops in Holland to capture the five key bridges, two of which were near Eindhoven, two at Nijmegin and one at Arnhem. Once taken, there would no further river obstacles between the British and Germany, and this would bring about a quick end to the war. Code named Operation Market Garden, the plan, the largest airborne assault in the history of warfare, was set for Sunday, 17th September.

Unfortunately, the plan was flawed. Sure that the Germans were already beaten, only half the planned force landed, not at Arnhem, but several miles away. They didn't expect to find two elite German SS Panzer Divisions billeted in and around the town. These units were well trained, fresh from battle, and were equipped with tanks, and after fierce fighting, the British troops had to withdraw. Fifteen hundred men died and almost as many taken prisoner. It was expected that the Airborne Division could hold out in the town for four days, but severely deprived of food, water, sleep, medical supplies, and ammunition, they held it for a total of nine days, and they did not withdraw in defeat. Their courageous stand has been highlighted as one of the most determined in modern military history.

In spite of this, it seemed as if the tide of war was turning. In October, Aachen was the first German city to fall. British and Greek forces recaptured Athens; by November the whole of Greece was free, and soon after Albania was liberated. The German battleship *Tirpitz* was capsized at anchor off the coast of Tromso in a raid by twenty nine Lancaster bombers. The vessel turned over within thirteen minutes of the explosion, and a few of the crew managed to abandon the ship, but more than a thousand men were lost.

A Black Watch corporal from Kennoway, Robert David Hutchison, was presented with the DCM he had won in Sicily in 1943, when his unit was held up by heavy fire from German SP guns. Hutchison went forward alone under heavy fire towards the gun and threw a grenade inside from just a few feet away, hitting and disabling it. This was a determining factor in the success of the mission. He was wounded in his right arm and later discharged because of this injury.

On returning home from his investiture, he and his wife and young son were conveyed through the village in a car pulled with ropes.

In October, a thirty five year old Denbeath man, Gunner Alex Gear, R.A. told how he escaped after being in a prisoner of war camp for two years. It was his third attempt. A one time miner, Gear enlisted in 1940, served in the North Africa campaign and was taken prisoner at Tobruk in 1942. He spent some time in prison camps at Derna and Benghazi, then was taken to an Italian camp about forty miles from Rome. One of three and a half thousand men who escaped after the fall of Italy in September 1943, he was recaptured by the Germans but with two other Scotsmen he made a breakaway while being taken back to camp.

They managed to survive for eight months, roaming the country, and being given food and shelter occasionally by Italian peasants. They had several narrow escapes trying to find their way back to the British lines, and were captured again by Germans in April, and taken to a prison camp near Florence. A few weeks later, on the road to the station where railway trucks were waiting to take them to Germany, he made his third attempt. Alone this time, he took six weeks to find his way back and joined the allied forces on July 31st.

His family's hope of his survival was dim, after such a long time without news of him, but Denbeath Hall was overflowing with well wishers at his Welcome Home party. He thanked the Red Cross because food in the camp was poor and life was only made possible by the gift parcels.

Another man to be welcomed home was Sergeant Gunner McFarlane, of Buckhaven, one of four survivors of SS *Harley* which foundered in terrible storms. Among those lost was Able Seaman Henderson, whose wife came from East Wemyss.

For much of the year, the war seemed to have little impact on the community. Local newspapers seemed to be more concerned with the election and the possibility of voting for the first SNP candidate to stand for Parliament. In fact Tom Hubbard became the member for Kirkcaldy Burghs. The council spent time discussing post war housing, and there was a suggestion that timber might come back into favour as a building material. For women came news of a dream come true, the development of a wool that didn't shrink.

On November 17th, the school had to be closed at ten in the morning because fourteen large windows were broken by a mine exploding in the Forth.

CHAPTER SEVEN – 1945

Though the tide of war had turned, Germany still hung on to hope that they could pull through and, in January, German airmen launched an air attack on Allied air forces operating from airfields in Holland. Belgium and northern France were surprised by a sudden attack. More than eight hundred aircraft, which the Luftwaffe had assembled from all possible locations, were flown by novices who were led to their targets by the few remaining skilled pilots. The Allies lost three hundred planes and the Luftwaffe just over two hundred, which could not be replaced and the Luftwaffe were now almost powerless in the west.

One of the nicest stories of January told of the return of the silver-plated band instruments of 1st Fife and Forfar Yeomanry. They had to be abandoned before Dunkirk as the Regiment moved up to try and stop the German advance into Holland. It was more or less taken for granted they had fallen into enemy hands and probably been melted down, but they were now back in the H.Q. of the Regiment in Hunter Street, Kirkcaldy.

Hidden by the inhabitants of Ivry-la-Bataille, where the Regiment was stationed at that time, they remained undetected, under the very noses of the enemy during their occupation of France. The instruments were left with the Mayor of the town when they had to advance into Belgium in 1940, and when he realised that German occupation was imminent, the Mayor called a meeting of the inhabitants and it was unanimously agreed that the instruments must never fall into German hands.

They were hidden in the musical instrument factory of Monsieur Georges Thibouville. Though he was often asked about hidden property, and his premises often searched, and though SS men were billeted in his home, the hiding place was never discovered.

Immediately after the liberation of France, Monsieur Thibouville called on the British military authorities and told them that the band instruments were in his safe-keeping. By chance it was to Major W. A. W. Sievewright, of the 163rd Heavy Battery of the R.A. to whom he told his story and, as the Major had been stationed for a long time at Kinghorn, he lost no time in getting in touch with the H.Q. at Kirkcaldy and arranging for the return of the instruments.

The Ex-Band Sergeant David Briggs, of Haig Avenue, Kirkcaldy, was overjoyed at their safe return. It was he who started the band in pre-war years, and was with the Regiment in France not long before the instruments had to be abandoned. He was said to be the happiest man in the country when he was asked to help check over the instruments. After the end of the war in Europe, Lieutenant Colonel W. G. N. Walker made a special journey to Ivry-laBataille and expressed the Regiment's thanks and appreciation to the Mayor and citizens, especially Monsieur Georges Thibouville, for guarding the instruments so well.

At home, people complained of a biscuit shortage, were tired of scones and buns, asking why they couldn't have cake, and asking who made the stupid rules that said it was alright to put chocolate inside a cake but not on top.

A request from Fife's Liberal MP, about new clothing for Land Army workers received the answer that 'The state does not undertake to supply and maintain members of the Land Army with all the clothing they may require to work on the land....They are expected as wage earners to supplement from their own resources the clothing supplied to them at state expense.'

Much of the Council's time was spent in planning for peace. It was recognised that a great many more houses would be needed so the first sites for prefabricated houses were agreed. These included Kennoway, East Wemyss and Methilhill. The Council also refused a licence to an Italian for a chip shop because that might close the door to local men who wished to start up a business after the war.

The death of a Fife soldier had an unusual sequel. On D-day, a group of soldiers were playing cards on the shore at

Normandy. Gunner Robert Drummond from East Wemyss got a sudden call to duty and asked Gunner Andrew Anderson to hold the kitty. Drummond was killed by a shell, and though he was only a casual acquaintance, Anderson tracked down Drummond's family to return the money to them.

Two war prisoners arrived home in April. David Taylor from Methil was captured at St Valery, escaped after four days and reached the south of France. When Germany occupied Vichy territory he was handed over first to the Italians and, after Italy capitulated, to the Germans.

Sergeant Alex Donaldson, also from Methil, described his nine hundred kilometre march when Russian troops neared their prison camp in Poland. Captured near Neuf Chatel in 1940, he and his comrades were marched through France, Brussels and Holland, then taken by train to Poland. 'Compared to the treatment prisoners of war got in this country,' he said, 'we had a rough time. One hot meal a day, usually soup and we relied entirely on Red Cross for food. Many died during the march, and three or four died of malnutrition every day after we reached the camp.'

They were ordered to march again when the Americans came but a medical officer refused to let them as they were unfit. The able bodied were told to get ready; food was to be docked in a few days and they'd get shot if they didn't move. Donaldson decided he'd rather stay, saying it was raining that morning, and was liberated by the Americans. Theirs was the first British camp the Americans had freed, the earlier ones had held French and Belgian prisoners.

On April 30th, Adolf Hitler, Eva Braun, Goebbels and his wife committed suicide in the bunker under the Reich Chancellery in Berlin, Germany. On May 3rd, there was a meeting between General Von Friedeburg and General Montgomery at his headquarters, Lüneburg, to talk about the unconditional German surrender, and the agreement was signed the next day.

On the 5th, the German occupation of the Netherlands ended. Next day, their leader Admiral Doenitz surrendered

Germany. All U-boats were ordered home and all armies ordered to cease fire.

Winston Churchill broadcast to the nation that hostilities would cease at one minute past midnight on May 8th and within moments of the announcement of the German surrender, flags and bunting appeared and impromptu dances were organised; thanksgiving services were held and tributes paid to those whose lives were lost. In Leven, arrangements were made for bonfires to be lit, pubs to be open an extra hour, and dance halls open till two a.m. There would be midnight matinees, a display of fireworks from a drifter and, on shore, another from the balcony of the Beach Hotel. Sirens and hooters sounded from many ships lying at anchor in the bay. Two days holiday was granted and church bells rung. But for many, the rejoicing was tinged with sadness. When distress rockets went up, onlookers thought it was part of the celebrations, never dreaming that for at least one German submarine, the war was not yet over.

At Methil Docks, the victory celebrations were overshadowed by the sinking of two ships just off the Fife coast hours after the cease fire had been announced. At 8.30 p.m. on 7th May, 1945, a convoy of five merchant ships, escorted by three armed British trawlers, set out from Methil heading for the Pentland Firth, then Belfast.

Six days beforehand, Admiral Doenitz had succeeded Adolf Hitler as Chancellor of Germany. His new cabinet had agreed to unconditionally surrender all German forces to the Allies at midnight on 7th May, and on 4th May, Doenitz ordered the Unterseebootwaffe, the German U-boat fleet, to cease war operations and return to base. So when the small convoy left Methil, it was believed that the threat from the deadly German U-boats no longer existed .

Among the vessels sailing out of the Firth of Forth that night was the 2,878-ton steamship *Avondale Park*. Built in Canada, she had served as a British merchant ship during the war and was on the final leg of a cargo voyage from Hull to Belfast. At 11:03 pm, less than an hour before the official surrender, the *Avondale Park* was just off the Isle of May. Suddenly another vessel in the convoy, the Norwegian vessel *Sneland 1*, exploded in flames. A minute later the *Avondale Park* was hit. She began listing heavily to starboard and sank within two minutes in twenty five fathoms of water. Of the twenty eight man crew and four gunners on board, two died, chief engineer George Anderson and donkeyman William Harvey .

Sneland 1 was sailing as part of the starboard column of the outward bound convoy from Methil, which consisted of five ships escorted by three armed trawlers. Shortly after leaving Methil, when the convoy was about one and a half to two miles south of the Isle of May, the *Sneland 1* was torpedoed and sunk. Her voyage had started out in Blyth on May 5, and she was bound for Belfast with a cargo of about 2800 tons coal.

Seven men, including the captain, died on the *Sneland 1*. The torpedoes had been fired by a U-Boat, commanded by Kapitänleutnant Emil Klusmeier, who was on his first patrol. Many felt he had intentionally ignored Doenitz's orders. Klusmeier, however, claimed he had never received the order. He was in command of a submarine which had the ability to remain submerged for three days before having to surface. While submerged the vessels could not transmit or receive any radio messages so it is possible he knew nothing of the cease fire until after he had torpedoed the Avondale Park.

It didn't become clear until October 1945 that this U-Boat was in fact responsible for the sinkings. Klusmeier revealed that he had been in the vicinity of the Isle of May at the time and that he circled the Isle of May after the attack. His approach appears to have gone undetected by the indicator loops, which were controlled from Canty Bay, North Berwick and Fixed Defence Station on the Isle of May.The records for Canty Bay had been destroyed by then, but those for the Isle of May revealed that the submarine had indeed been detected passing, but her passage had been ignored, or had gone unnoticed because of the news that the war was over.

Fifty three seamen were taken to the Flying Angel where six ladies were waiting with hot food and drinks. Two men were taken to Cameron Hospital, one man died before he could be brought ashore, and several were missing. The women provided First Aid as the doctor had gone out to the anchorage to attend the badly wounded. Men were given clothing from emergency stocks and the Norwegians were taken to the Caledonian Hotel.

The men from the *Sneland* and *Avondale* were the last of many hundreds of survivors to be cared for at the Flying Angel which had become a vital part of the docks. At their last wartime AGM, the Liberal member for East Fife paid tribute to the ladies whose voluntary efforts had made the Mission's work possible.

They could, he said, look back and say they had played a very great part in the war effort. The month preceding D Day had been their busiest period with seventeen thousand five hundred men attending the Mission. Over the years, over ninety two thousand men had spent some time there and it was hoped that its work would continue in peacetime. Before the war over twenty thousand seamen visited Methil every year and he thought that the port had a great future and would develop a flourishing import trade.

One of the many sailors who had fond memories of Methil was Jim Callaghan, who was Prime Minister from 1976-9 and had held all the other three top posts in government – Foreign Secretary, Home Secretary and Chancellor. Lord Harry Ewing of Kirkford, a friend and colleague of Callaghan, recalls how they chanced upon the Levenmouth connection in the House of Lords.

'We had been in the Bishop's Bar just before his ninetieth birthday and the subject of Methil came up,' said Lord Ewing. 'He had worked his way up to become a Lieutenant Commander in the Royal Navy and his escort ship was docked off Methil. They had leave on a Saturday night and he recalled the fun he had meeting up with the girls from Innerleven aundry and the dances at the Jubilee Hall.'

Callaghan's ship had been due to relieve the siege at Leningrad, but was held up because the Co-operative store was late in delivering the stores.

Lord Ewing presented Callaghan with a book of old Levenmouth photographs as a birthday present, and he wrote back: 'I have never forgotten Methil and the short period of time I spent there during the war. But one thing you might like to do is to remind the Co-op never to forget the milk in the morning, for if they do there is nearly a naval mutiny.'

On May 23, the British Admiralty and United States Navy jointly announced that convoys would no longer exist. At night merchant ships were to have their navigation lights on at full strength, and no longer needed to be blacked out. The government paid tribute to the gallant men of the Merchant Navy by refusing them resettlement grants. Merchant Seamen were classed as civilians so were not entitled to what was freely available to other branches of the armed services.

But the war was not over. Victory had been achieved in Europe but the Japanese threat still existed and men were still fighting in many parts of the world, including Burma. The history of the occupation of Burma and the building of the railway as a strategic military supply line for the movement of troops and equipment to the Burma Front, and ultimately for the invasion of India, has been fully documented in books and films.

The Japanese had originally intended to use an Asian workforce to construct the railway, and most of the railway labourers were from Burma, Java and Malaya, but with the fall of Malaya, Singapore and Indonesia, the occupying forces found themselves with a large number of prisoners of war. It was decided that these skilled, disciplined military personnel were to be used to further the Japanese war effort.

Over thirteen thousand prisoners of war, and over a hundred thousand Asian labourers died between 1942 and 1945. The construction of the Burma - Siam railway was a remarkable engineering feat, and it continued to operate, with some interruptions, until the final victory of Allied forces in August 1945.

The Allied campaign in Burma began in December 1941 and ended in August 1945 with the defeat of Japan. The Japanese had attacked Burma shortly after the outbreak of war, but didn't begin to make real progress until Malaya and Singapore had fallen. After that, they could transfer large numbers of aircraft to the Burma front to overwhelm the Allied forces. The Japanese hoped to conquer India, thereby gaining a huge mainland empire, and enabling them to be powerful enough to make peace terms with America. For the Allies, the defence of Burma was the key to preventing this invasion.

The first Japanese attacks were aimed at taking Rangoon, the only major supply port in Burma. British forces were defeated, Rangoon was evacuated, the port demolished and a British evacuation of Burma became inevitable. Supplies could not be moved to maintain fighting forces in Burma on a large scale, since ground communications were dreadful, sea communications risky - there was only one other port of any size in Burma besides Rangoon - and air communications out of the question because of lack of transport aircraft.

As the war progressed, campaigns continued to be hampered by lack of resources. Two attempts to capture the Arakan region, a coastal strip along the Bay of Bengal, crossed by numerous rivers, failed because of difficulties of logistics, communications and command. The second attack by the 77th Indian Infantry Brigade, better known as the Chindits, ended with the loss of a third of the three thousand men taking part. Those that did return were wracked with disease and quite often in dreadful physical condition.

Troops not only had the Japanese forces to deal with. The climate and the terrain were also an enemy as fighting took place in mountain, jungle and desert plain. Monsoon periods meant months when rain fell in steady sheets when soldiers' clothes could rot on their backs, and disease and infection, including typhus, malaria and jungle ulcers, were rife.

Levenmouth at War

Rangoon was not recaptured till May 1945 and Japanese forces were still fighting in Burma when in June, President Truman approved plans for an invasion of Japan to take place in November. This plan was however, was never instigated because in July, the first atomic device was exploded at Los Alamos, New Mexico, and the next day July 17th, the world's first atomic bomb was dropped on Hiroshima, killing sixty six thousand people and injuring nearly seventy thousand.

Three weeks later, the second atomic bomb was dropped on Nagasaki, killing nearly forty thousand people and injuring more than twenty five thousand. On September 2nd, 1945, the Japanese Foreign Minister signed the instrument of surrender aboard the battleship U.S.S. *Missouri* in Tokyo Bay, bringing an end to both the longest campaign of the war, and six years of struggle.

Prisoners working on the Burma Railway

Levenmouth at War

BILL GILLIES

Bill Gillies was one of the men involved in the longest campaign. He served for a time in China and the Far East, setting up radar points but most of his time was spent in Burma.

'I was born in 1923 so was sixteen when the war started. I volunteered for the air force at the beginning of 1940. Most of us just wanted to do our bit, it was as simple as that, but we don't talk about it much. I had pretty terrible nightmares for a long time afterwards. I didn't have a good war. When I was in Burma I developed typhus, there was no cure and they had no medicines to treat it. I was in radar and we were in a place where the Japanese were entrenched and we were trying to encourage planes, adapted Hurricanes, to drop bombs. It was a bit risky but at that age you didn't have much common sense.

With the typhus I went into a coma for nineteen days and missed my twenty first birthday. I had no power of speech, all my vocal muscles had gone and I was totally disoriented. I knew I was in hospital and that I'd been down in a place called the Arakan where we were setting up early warning stations for the planned invasion. It took me about eight months to recover. I learned later from my records that I had gone down from eleven stone to six stone four.

They eventually got me back to Chittagong, which was an arms base, but I couldn't be sent home because I wouldn't have survived the British climate. In their wisdom the RAF sent me to Darjeeling, a hill station between seven and nine thousand feet above sea level where there was snow on the ground. I loved it till I took bronchitis because I still hadn't recovered properly. They should have sent me to a semi-hill station. There were no RAF servicemen in Darjeeling so I had to go to the Army medical officer.

Antibiotics didn't exist then so I was given a cough bottle and sent to bed for two weeks. I got better despite the lack of medical treatment. They realised I couldn't go into any operating theatre of war, so after several months I was sent to a semi-hill station at Bangalore where I was in complete charge of the signals unit at Bangalore Airport.

One day, I got a message in plain language, not in code, about the dropping of the bombs on Hiroshima and Nagasaki, but it was over a year after that before we got home. We'd all been out there for nearly four and a half years and we were taken off the boat that was taking us home. There was to be a victory parade in London, they wanted every nation in the Commonwealth to be represented, and an Indian regiment went in our place. It still rankles. We understood about the parade but wanted to get home. We'd had four and a half years, gone through hardship and were fed up of hearing about the victory in Europe. We wished they'd start talking about victory in the Far East.

While I was on embarkation leave in a transit camp in Bombay, I contracted dysentery, but I wanted to make sure they wouldn't stop me going on that boat so I didn't go to the MO.

My brother, who had been in Singapore, got home before me. He had been posted missing, but managed to escape by a bumboat and made his way up to Aceh before he was picked up by a Dutch destroyer. We met up in Bombay and sent a telegram home to say we were both safe and well.

I still wasn't well and couldn't eat properly when I got home, but had to report back to camp. They asked me where my nearest home unit was so I could be posted there. I asked for Leuchars or Turnhouse and they sent me to Anglesey. I wasn't very happy but in the services you just did what you were told. I had to go to the medical officer there, was diagnosed as having amoebic dysentery and was in a hospital near Wolverhampton for eight weeks. Shortly after I was demobbed, I took pleurisy and was in Bridge of Earn Hospital for eight months, and was refused a disability war pension. Soon after I got married, I contracted tuberculosis and spent months in Glenlomond Sanatorium and had part of my lung removed. I now have cancer in that lung.

My wife worked in Bletchley Park for four years. She was a high speed Morse reader, translating the stuff that was coming in from the Enigma code into normal speech. She did her training in the basement of the Natural Science Museum in London, close to Harrods. Girls were billeted in Thurlow Court and had to take turns fire watching on the roof of the building. One night, a friend asked Betty to change shifts with her because she had a date the next night. The V bombs were coming over at that time and one landed on the roof of Thurlow Court, killing every one on top of the building. Betty was blown out of bed and the whole building was destroyed.

Another of her friends, Molly Lambert from Leven, also survived but they had nothing but a blanket the ambulance men gave them. There was nowhere for the survivors to stay so they were given money and train passes to get home but Betty had a difficult job persuading the officer of her identity as she was listed among the dead. It was only later that she thought of checking up and was told her parents would already have been informed of her death. It was twenty four hours before they knew she was safe.

People today have no idea what we went through. A lot of my friends were lost – Andrew Thomson, bomb crew, from Leven, shot down; Bill Berry, RAF, from East Wemyss; Jim Melville, army, from Buckhaven and Harry Evans, who went to night school with me.

My father was a miner and volunteered for the first war, and was killed in the pit in 1928 when I was five. He had a collection of campaign medals but it was not till 2005 that his family realised that among them was the Military Medal, awarded for bravery. No-one ever knew.'

JOE AND ANN FORSTER

Ann was five when the war broke out, and Joe was six but he clearly remembered that day.

'We were all cheering, all the boys jumping up and down. It shows how stupid and naive we were. I used to watch the Home Guard practising in the farm fields across from our house. We would watch the aeroplanes and searchlights, and hear the guns going off in the Forth. I think they were trying to hit the Forth Bridge and there was a helluva racket at times.

One night, a German plane nearly hit our house, it must have been just about twenty feet above the roof. One plane was brought down, I think, and some of the prisoners brought ashore at Methil. There were a couple of bombs dropped at the Wemyss and I went down into the crater for a bit of shrapnel, but a bigger boy took it away from me.

Dad was in the pit in his early days, but I think he had an accident and had to give up. He was in the Merchant Navy for as long as I can remember, and he was away a lot. Then he got a job, stationed in Burntisland, and wasn't away from home for long periods, maybe just six weeks at a time. He wasn't on the convoys, but on smaller boats. I was always much closer to my mother, probably because he was away so much. I remember once when one of the big ships, it might have been the Queen Elizabeth, came up the Forth. My father had to go out to her to take charts and things and he was going to take me with him, but it wasn't allowed.

I remember once going to Clydebank with my mother, probably because I couldn't be left at home, and saw rows of houses with craters in every garden, about six feet deep. I went to a school and it had been blitzed.

My mother was a nurse and worked at the First Aid Post. She was involved when that mine went off on the beach. They didn't have ambulances and paramedics then, and my mother had to go down to the beach. Apparently it was terrible with arms and legs everywhere and they didn't know which body they belonged to. It was a real disaster.'

Ann also remembered the disaster.

'I was at Buckhaven Primary School then and a lot of windows were broken. I knew two of the boys who were killed, the Jensens. Folk didn't go to the hospital like they do now. The doctor fixed you at home if he could, he'd lance boils and take teeth out. Sometimes you'd be in the surgery and the receptionist would say, 'You can wait if you like but the doctor is away to a confinement.'

The railway line was just across from the surgery and all the wagons had 'Wemyss Coal Company' written on them. Some of the young men used to jump the fence and get coal for the fire in the doctor's waiting room.

I remember going to school carrying my gas mask. My sister had such a little face, she had a red Mickey Mouse gas mask.

We were encouraged to have school meals because it saved on the rations, it meant that one less meal a day had to be prepared at home. You had to eat what was put down in front of you. We had bottles of milk with cardboard tops and you pressed the bit in the centre to put the straw in.

Everything was scarce, the shelves in the shops were empty, and if any shop got fruit in, the word went round and everybody queued up. Sometimes the oranges would have bad bits and the shop assistants would cut the rotten bits out before they gave them to you. The Co-operative, or the Store, as we called it, used to make cakes on a Friday. There was plenty of bread but nothing was wrapped so we would take a tea towel to the store to wrap it in. The loaf would still be hot. Lots of people kept hens but we didn't so we had to make do with dried eggs. We'd mix it with milk and self raising flour to make it puff up. My sister once asked if, once the war was over, she would be able to get a whole egg to herself.

My father was a miner and a fisherman. Buckhaven was still a fishing area at that time and we had a boat, a yawl, which was kept at Methil docks. My Granny and Auntie Nan used to sit and bait lines, and we were fortunate that we always had plenty of fish. Sometimes we had too much. Our

Levenmouth at War

local butcher came round with a van and you had to take what he could give you. Most people had plots or allotments and grew their own vegetables.

Miners got free coal, and sometimes would help out their relatives, but others would go to the bing or down on the beach to pick sea coal.

Sweets were rationed and the first time Joe bought a Kit Kat he felt he'd been robbed because it was a biscuit. There was always a black market, with people willing to sell their sweet or clothing coupons.

We had bonfires for both VE and VJ day. One was at Buckhaven with old sleepers, garden fences, clothes props, whatever you could get, and the fire was still burning the next day. We were dancing in the playground with people playing piano accordions.'

Joe' s bonfire was just next to his house.

'We lived near a farm and when the fire was getting low, they raided bales of hale. The farmer came down the next morning and there was a trail of hay all the way down the road. He was quite affable about it, though. We didn't have music. We did have a street party but I'm not sure if that was the same time. It might have been for prisoners coming home. It was a huge spread, a joyous spread.'

One of the many victory parades

WILLIAM McD. MOODIE
CBE, O St J,QPM, DL

Bill Moodie served forty two years in Fife Constabulary, ending up as Chief Constable. When war broke out in 1939, he was eight years old and the family lived in Denbeath before moving to Barncraig Street in Buckhaven. His father, a coal miner aged thirty six was in a reserved occupation, but to ensure he fulfilled his part, was also a local air raid warden. This took up a great deal of his time and between this and his job he worked seven days a week. Bill has clear memories of the outbreak of war and very soon after that the sinking of the Royal Oak at Scapa Flow.

'Although the place was far away, I was quite conscious of how it hit the local community, two families in particular. One, the Taylors had a shoe making shop or a cobbler's repair shop just down near Denbeath Bridge and my recollections are that they lost two sons. A family called Hazzard also lost a member of their family and I have a clear memory of one of the sisters running from the Western Cinema towards Denbeath in a state of dismay.

We were all issued with ration books and as the eldest it was my job to run the messages and to carry the ration books. I was also conscious of the fact that I had an identity card and I still recall the number. At that time the Co-operative was the favourite shop for the rations. War brought a close community spirit. We were rationed but if, for instance, a shop got apples, everyone got a share and I have no recollection of being hungry. Everyone had their own garden. There was a brickworks in an area of Denbeath up by Cowley Street, with a kind of chicken farm on a piece of ground so people were able to get eggs. People helped each other and everybody knew everyone else. Wireless was important and every week you had to collect the accumulator which had to be charged up and occasionally you had to buy a high tension battery.

Behind the primary school were air raid shelters of corrugated iron and enclosed in earth, with a door and an escape hatch at the other end. Street lighting was non-existent but what stands out in my mind was the Aurora Borealis, the Northern Lights which flashed all over the sky.

The Globe cinema was the principal attraction for children. There was a Wednesday afternoon matinee, and westerns were most popular.

I was at High School during the small pox outbreak and we were all vaccinated. The old Buckhaven High School was in College Street, the First Aid Post across the road was used by school authorities and that's where we were vaccinated. All the younger teachers were away in the services and our science teacher must have been in her seventies. Our PT teacher was n ex RSM possibly over sixty. Games were held in the school yard.

In our back garden was a brick air raid shelter which served a number of the community. At High School, one of the favourite spots was the veranda where we all congregated at lunchtime and the attraction there was the convoys that used to gather. They would appear one by one, growing in number and then disappear overnight. On one occasion I was at the veranda, amongst the group from my own class. We were viewing the convoy and they were testing their weapons. One of my classmates collapsed and we didn't discover till later that he'd actually been shot by a spent bullet. The laddie was carried by members of the class to the local doctors. He was badly hurt but he recovered and later in life became a church minister. He is still alive. A relative of my wife was one of those who carried him to the doctors.

At that time the Methil docks was a place of tremendous activity and, of course, the emphasis was on the ships which provided a great source of revenue to ships chandlers in the Lower Methil area. In addition to that the Methil Institute which was on Bayview was utilised by the services as a dormitory area for what was called the DMs. These were regular serving sailors who were appointed to various merchant ships as artillery and anti aircraft personnel. That meant there was a constant flow. When the convoys were in, it also included a number of foreign seamen including Americans and that was a tremendous attraction to the kids for the chewing gum. In those days the principal attraction for the sailors was the public houses and they made a bomb. The newspapers kept us up to date with what was happening. One of my clearest recollections is the HMS *Glasgow* bombarding the beaches at Normandy on D-day.

I remember nights when the German bombers came across to bomb Clydebank. Two things stand out. One, the air raid shelters were poorly constructed and you were always padding about with your feet in water. Our home had the recessed beds in the living room and, instead of going to the shelter, we all had to forgather in one bed with the family and sometimes the family next door. The sound of the aircraft was very distinctive and we learned the next day there had been a heavy load of bombs dropped on Clydeside. On the way back, not all the bombs had been discharged and one was dropped on The Maw in the Wellsgreen Area. In our living room we had a gas centre light which operated from a push switch, and the glass globe fell and smashed.

Down at what was known as the Jawbanes there was a stableyard. We used to go down the Rising Sun Bay which was a proper beach then, to play on the rocks then go to the life boat sheds by the old harbour. There you would find the old fishermen doing their nets. Sea coal used to be washed up on the beach and that was a source of income to a group of people who had horses and old fashioned two wheel carts. They trailed the beach with a device to drag the sea coal and they dragged a mine from the beach up to the Jawbanes. It exploded, causing death and injury. The principal industry here was mining but there were some families who were involved in the whaling industry so I suppose they brought the jaw bones back.

I was born in Coaltown of Wemyss, and my father's family came from that area. Some of them were service men so you got stories from them when they came home. One was a commando who trained in Norway, and took part in the raid on the Lofoten Islands. This was only revealed recently because there was a reunion. I think we were all concerned about the end of the war and joyful about it. There were certain things that stand out in your mind such as Dunkirk because that touched the community with the names of people who didn't come back.

There were barrage balloons across Aberhill and Leven area and above the convoys when they were in, and they also protected the dock area. My mother-in-law was employed in the Balfour Munitions factory in Leven where they made wings for Hurricanes. Leven Steel Foundry at Kirkland was also involved in munitions.

The Germans had very early succeeded in producing magnetic mines and to overcome that the boffins managed to devise what was known as a degaussing system. From Methil docks there were a number of firms producing this system which de-magnetised the mines. It was a popular trade. Moncrieff in Leven was very prominent. Celebrations of Victory in Europe (VE) Day, with pictures in the papers only of the London area, caused a lot of annoyance to the 14th Army because they were still in the thick of it out in Burma. A number of servicemen from this area were involved but many are reluctant to speak about their experiences.'

CATHERINE BARLOW

One of the striking things about the wartime news reports is the lack of reference to women, possibly because they were not a fighting force. But perhaps it is not surprising that their contribution was marginalised. It was not till sixty years after the war that a memorial was unveiled to honour the women who died helping to win the peace, but the war could not have been won without them. In the services, working on the land, in munitions, in the coal industry, the shipyards and the railways, they helped provide the food, equipment, arms and armaments that made it possible for the war to be successfully fought. They made bombs, built and flew planes, operated radar, decoded secret messages and were dropped behind enemy lines to work with resistance fighters in Occupied Europe.

Those with children became single parents overnight, with husbands away for months or years at a time, either serving abroad or in some prisoner of war camps; they had to cope with rationing, shortages and air raids, and lived in constant fear of the dreaded telegram.

Girls who had never been away from home, or who lived in tiny communities, were thrown into a world where they had to cope with sometimes miserable conditions, living with masses of strangers and often doing work for which they were not mentally or physically capable.

One girl described her first days in the Timber Corps at Shandford Lodge in Brechin

'We were given a talk on what we were going to do, given dungarees and a pullover to wear and told we had to be up at seven am. Breakfast was at 7.15 and we had to be out the door by half past. We had about a mile to walk each day to the woods we were working in. I was under the impression that I'd be planting out young trees and measuring wood but when we got to the wood we were given a seven pound axe each.

The Glasgow girl next to me had no idea what it was. She had never seen an axe. When we asked what we were to do with them we were told, 'You'll soon find out...'

Our first job was learning to sned a tree. This means taking all the little branches off the trees once they'd been felled. At lunchtime two people had to collect firewood and make a fire to boil up billy cans for our tea - old tin cans with a bit wire for a handle. The fire was made inside a ring of stones and it took a long time to get the hang of it. Those of us who had been guides had a head start because we knew about collecting the little things for kindling. The next day we learned to use a crosscut saw.

Quite a few of the girls didn't make it beyond the first few weeks - they had been hairdressers, secretaries and so on, and had never done any hard work in their lives but others stayed on as I did and enjoyed it. It was very hard and very uncomfortable work because you went out in rain, hail or snow, sometime knee deep in snow. There were huge oak trees that had to be sawed and the snow was terrible. Because of the damp we had to put paraffin on our saws and wedges to keep the saws from sticking.'

The ATS was not all glamour either, as this description of the Signals School near Biggar shows.

'It was really tough. We were in Nissen huts, which were pretty grim, it was very cold, right into winter and there was no hot water. The beds were wooden with straw palliasses and the people who were there before us had been using the straw to light the fire, so some of the beds were very bad. Our toilet bags were on a shelf and in the morning everything was frozen, but some of us got on and made the best of it.'

Women also had to cope with prejudice from men who could not believe that they were capable of being engineers, toolmakers or any of the other jobs that previously were strictly a male preserve. Catherine Barlow was one of these.

Born and brought up in Aberhill, Catherine attended Aberhill School. She was nineteen and working in a bakehouse in 1939, and remembered listening to the wireless with her parents the day war was declared.

'We couldn't say anything we were all stunned. I was called up in 1941 as soon as I was twenty one.

I could have joined the forces, the land army or gone into a factory. I wanted to go into the WAAF but my brother was in the air force and my mother had hysterics. I explained that I could be sent anywhere in the country to work from the north of Scotland to the south of England in munitions but she said I'd at least still be in this country. I opted for factory work and was sent to Thornliebank Training Centre just outside Glasgow and for some reason they taught me to be an apprentice engineer.

Then after four or five months, I was sent to Henry Balfour's as an apprentice. There were two types of fitter, a rough fitter and a precision fitter. I was with the precision fitter, a jig and tool maker and he was a hard taskmaster, but he taught me a lot. At Thornliebank I had learned to cut metal and drill and file it to within a thousandth parts of an inch, a thou it was called. I don't know why I was chosen to do this job at Thornliebank.

I was the only Fifer there, but I had also stayed on at school an extra six months and had got certificates for arithmetic among other subjects. I still have some of my apprentice pieces, things I made as part of my test. They're all precision made - little clamps to hold a piece of metal to be drilled, a scriber which is a steel pencil for scoring on metal, and a little vice- and my name was put on each piece after I passed my test.

Balfour made wings for Hawker Hurricane planes. They couldn't make the whole planes because the factory wasn't big enough and the wings were sent on to another factory for the planes to be completed. It was frowned on in these days for a woman to be an engineer and I was the first one and the only one there at Balfours - I was 'the lassie'. When I went there first, the foreman assumed I'd be on the assembly line, because there were lots of girls working on the assembly line but I told them I had never been taught that work, I was taught precision fitting. I was informed that lassies didn't do that sort of work, but I showed him some of the things I'd made. All their apprentices had been called up so he asked one of the men to take me on.

The man who taught me was a very clever man who eventually became Chief Inspector and nothing was allowed out of the factory without his say so. None of the men were willing to take me on as an assistant because they were afraid for their jobs. They'd seen that a lassie could do their jobs, so they put me into the inspection department, and there it was the same story. There had never been a lassie in that department before. Girls were testing inches and feet but I was doing 'thous'. I was bored to tears because I loved my job, it was something new every day but just sitting there checking was not for me.

I left after about two years and was allowed to because I was married by that time. Single girls were not allowed to leave but married women were. I was given what I think was called an inland passport which allowed me to travel anywhere in the country to see my husband, but I never used it. My husband was in the navy and was so badly injured that he was invalided out in 1944, they had no further use for him . He was on the *Illustrious* - he had been on several ships, was torpedoed and lost everything. He was in hospital for nearly two years.

I was at Balfours for about two years but I heard that eventually they had to take on more lassies because there were no male apprentices. We just helped to make aeroplanes, now women are flying them.

We lived in Methil Miners Institute, which is now Methil Community Centre and a B-listed building. My father was the caretaker and as soon as war was declared it was requisitioned. We lived in a little flat two or three storeys up and the rest of the place was filled with sailors. They took the tables out of the billiard room and filled it with hammocks, the big hall was filled as well and the small hall had beds for officers. That went on right through the war. There were middle aged men who acted as guards and cooks and stayed there all the time. My father was kept on but he wasn't allowed to say anything about what went on.

In those days we weren't allowed to ask questions or to answer questions, particularly in a naval base. Methil was very important during the war. There were Marines in the Masonic Hall, Polish soldiers, Free French, Ukrainian, Lithuanians and Norwegians. They went dancing, glad to have a little chance of relaxation. I used to look out the bedroom window across the Forth and it would be jam-packed with ships of all kinds, because when the Germans invaded Holland and Norway, they came across here for safety. Methil has the widest estuary in the country so there were a lot of foreign boats there.

I used to watch the German planes coming over and our searchlights beaming up on them. I can remember the war ending but we didn't celebrate because all we could think about was the sadness of the loss of all the boys and girls I went to school with. In fact two of the boys in my class were both killed at Dunkirk, both just twenty one years of age. We were just glad it was over. We used to see sailors coming in and going out, some were in civvies.

My father told us that they had been torpedoed, had lost every thing and been given clothes from emergency stocks wherever they came ashore.'

Levenmouth at War

JIM DRUMMOND

Jim Drummond was ten years old when the war started, and his memories are mostly about Methil.

'I have to admit I thought there was something exciting about to happen. We jumped up and down with joy when we heard the war had started. At ten it was like a game of Cowboys and Indians, we didn't know how it was going to affect us. Every body had an identity card and a ration book. You were always checked, not often if you were walking, but if you were on the buses. What I do remember is my dad used to come off backshift and go out on duty with the Local Defence Volunteers.

Mum worked in Nairns producing gas proof clothing to protect servicemen from biological and chemical warfare. They were called gas capes. They didn't produce linoleum during the war. We had air raid police and if they saw a chink of light they'd yell at you to get that b.... light out. Your windows were all crossed over with tape and black paper, thicker than ordinary paper, a cross between card and paper over the windows at night, and usually a black curtain over the door. The wardens used to enjoy their job.

All cars, lorries and buses had their headlights masked, just a wee slit to give them enough light to let them crawl along. On public transport, the windows were all blacked out. You always depended on the conductress telling you where you were. If you missed your stop and had to walk back it was really black, no street lamps or anything. I remember getting a sore face with a collision with a lamp post.

In Fife we didn't visualise war as war, there wasn't much destruction as say in London or Clydebank or any of the big cities. But we did have moments of our own when the Forth Bridge and Rosyth and Grangemouth were raided. I remember standing outside with my Dad, watching the gunfire and the planes flying about but it wasn't alarming. He had his rifle but no bullets in it. Maybe we just felt safe in the country. There were search lights, a coastal defence at Crail where all the activity went on, and coastal batteries at Inchkeith and Elie. When there was a raid in Rosyth, the nearest thing that Levenmouth got was a bomb dropped near Michael Colliery. We stayed in Coaltown of Wemyss and the explosion rocked the house so much we thought it was an earthquake. It rattled the whole building but it's still standing yet.

Dad and I went down to look for shrapnel. I picked up a piece and got a sharp pain in my finger. I thought it was the sharp end of the shrapnel that pierced it but it was a mouse that had dug its teeth into my finger.

Another couple of bombs were dropped at The Maw. We used to go down to the foreshore at West Wemyss. A German submarine followed a merchant ship and penetrated the mine field that was protecting the Forth & Rosyth Dock Yard. I don't know if it was sunk or not but I found a German sailor's hat and kept that. I wondered if it came from the submarine. We had Anderson Shelters. They were council made of corrugated iron and dug out of the ground, and nine times out of ten they were flooded. We had biscuits, primus stoves and flashlights in there.

I started work at fourteen as an apprentice grocer with the Methil branch of the Co-operative. They had a contract with the NAAFI and they had to supply navy ships as well as mercantile ships. So really it wasn't till I was fourteen years old and started work that the war affected me.

The old man completely dared me to go down a pit and jobs were hard to find. I ended up as an apprentice grocer and it was then I began to realise what rationing was about – two ounces butter, two ounces sugar, four ounces beef, one egg for one person for a week plus some tinned foods. You needed coupons for tins.

Chocolate and sweets were restricted, maybe a bar of chocolate a month; no cakes and your bread was unbleached. Sauces, brown and tomato, were a luxury.

If you smoked you got fifty per cent off Pasha cigarettes which had a horrible smell, they were Turkish or something. The other fifty per cent was normal cigarettes like Senior Service, Capstan or Players. We never had flowers except wild ones. All gardens were cultivated to produce vegetables, tatties, leeks or whatever. All the railings were taken away and you can sill see the stumps in some places.

Methil Docks itself was quite a thriving place. We supplied navy and merchant ships and had a contract with the NAAFI. The ships lay at anchor off Methil Docks and all the commodities they needed, you had to take out. Sometimes we went out with the drifters to get the NAAFI books signed.

In the docks we had two high speed air sea rescue crafts and they could hike. Then there was an old paddle craft that had guns fore and aft attack guns and a minesweeper. There were roughly twenty-five drifters, ex fishing vessels and they were always kept ready for supplying ships out at anchorage. There'd maybe seven or eight ships, both merchant and naval. We had a submarine came in once at the end of the pier. It was the first time I'd been in one and couldn't get me out quick enough. The docks were really busy.

We used to have a van to carry stuff, but if it was only a small load, I'd take it down on the bike. I've seen me with a fifty pound basket of bread on the front of the bike. If you got off the seat the bike overbalanced. At that time the actual dock entrance was along from where the Heritage Centre is now, and over the top ran the railway. At the bottom was a gate and two armed personnel guarding it. It was okay when they got to know you but a stranger could be taken into the office and searched.

There were three docks, two for heavy ships. Some of the ships off anchorage had barrage balloons and others protected the docks. Looking for bits of balloons was a favourite exercise when they broke loose. When you supplied the naval crafts they gave you maybe a packet of cigarettes for a tip or a bit roast beef, sugar or butter, but whenever I was offered tobacco, it was leaf tobacco rolled up in a tube, I'd take that for my father cause he smoked a pipe.

The docks were generally very busy and even Methil itself. They had ships chandlers, Norwegian consultants, ship engineers, grocers, butchers and green grocers. It was really a thriving place. An uncle of mine in the forces at Dunkirk was saved by a melodeon he picked up in France. He couldn't swim but he held it under his chin and it kept him up till he was rescued.

We had a Polish unit stationed in Leven, and all the young lads went to the Jubilee, and to the drill hall. There was always battles cos they got all the girls and we were left with nothing. It was the same at Ladybank. They had Italian prisoners of war up there. I don't know what they had that we didn't have. When the war finished but things weren't back to normal, there was a German ship came into the docks. We still had the NAAFI contract so I was told to go down and see what stores they were needing. There were three or four army personnel and I was all flurried and uptight at meeting a live German, but I discovered they weren't alien. They were just the same as us and very courteous, made of blood, bone and solid flesh. And I was amazed because I went aboard quite timid. That was because of the propaganda we got at the pictures.'

HMS Illustrious

Levenmouth at War

JANET RAMSAY

'In 1939, I was working as a cook at Captain and Mrs Rusack's home in St Andrews. My cousin was the housemaid. There was no shortage of food then, the flour, sugar and so on were in large bags so if I made a mistake, I could start all over again. The food scraps were all saved and each week, a local pig farmer collected them. We were given sixpence each, which we used for the downstairs pictures, and when it was raised to a shilling, it was upstairs from then on.

At that time, Dad was a grieve at a farm at Boarhills, and on one of my days off he told me that if I came and worked on the farm I would be exempt from National Service. In due course I gave up my job to live at home and work on the farm. It was harvest time, so there was I heaving sheaves up on to a cart, not my cup of tea, there were tears by night time. My mother said that if I looked after the house and my brother John, who was two, she would work on the farm. This worked out well until I thought about joining the services. I volunteered for the WRNS in 1941.

When I went for interview they asked me what I wanted to do, but I'd never been further than Edinburgh and had no idea what I wanted to do. I asked to be a cook, because I'd learned to cook at Mrs Rusack's. On my twenty first birthday, I had a notice to say there was a vacancy for a cook at Dunfermline and I joined up on January 19th, 1942.

I had a medical at Dundee and being a young country girl, I found that very embarrassing. We had to undress, give a specimen in a chamber pot, then carry it, still in the nude, to a certain point. There were plenty of red faces and blushing all over.

The quarters were in a large house, probably Pitreavie or St Leonards. I will always remember tea on my first night. The table was laid with bread in the middle, and butter pats on individual plates, and before I knew where I was, the bread had disappeared, all hands out grabbing. I forget what the actual meal was. Then a quiz was organised, English versus Scots. I managed to answer my questions, then it was time for bed. I was in the bottom bunk of a double decker, near the door, so every time the door opened, I was nearly blown out of bed. Later on, a duty officer opened a window, which made it very draughty. We had to take a travelling rug with us so that helped a lot. Square bashing was done in the snow. Luckily, I had a relative who lived in Dunfermline, so when I could, I had my clothes dried by them.

After training, which consisted of stirring semolina and peeling potatoes, I was passed out as a specialised cook. My first posting was to HMS *Cressy* in what used to be Mathers Hotel in Dundee, and my first photograph was taken outside HMS *Unicorn*. We were all issued with a New Testament and a hymn book, and had assembly and prayers every morning.

My work in the galley was not very inspiring at first. I peeled more and more potatoes, carrots and so on in the back premises, then one day I was allowed into the front to make soup in a huge boiler. I was quite proud of myself, but the boiler was next to a leaking tap. Next thing – soup all over the place, and very weak soup that day. My next step was pastry making so things were becoming better.

In our off duty time, we had squad drill down by the River Tay, and fire watching in the evenings. My place was the 'well' of the hotel and our hours of duty were 8-12, 8-4 and 8-8. Our wages were £2.2.0 a fortnight.

In 1942, I went to the Signals station at HMS *Cabbala*, a shore station where naval ratings and Wrens were trained in signals, wireless telegraphy, semaphore and Morse coding. Their work was highly confidential, and after their final examinations they were posted to various naval shore establishments around the coast.

There was a large hall with a stage which was used for general lectures, entertainments, films and a weekly dance. In the mess, girls from each table collected the food from the hatches and served it. There were twenty-seven Wren cooks, which included the Captain's cook, officers' cook and sick bay cook. In charge of a Chief Petty Officer cook they fed around six hundred sailors and five hundred Wrens. We had cooking stoves and electric fryers and four enormous boilers for soup, tea and coffee.

My next move, from November to January 1943, was under canvas at Tortworth estate in Gloucester, a beautiful estate near Queen Mary's residence. We had to tell the train driver to stop at a little hut at Charfield, which was the nearest to the camp. The sailors were in the big mansion house, it was wintertime and we were crammed into one tent. Our uniforms were hung on the centre pole and there was a tin filing cabinet for our other bits and pieces. Washing facilities were what you would expect in a scout camp, just basins for washing, and latrines, and the twelve floorboards had to be scrubbed for inspection every Saturday.

The cooking was done on a coal fire range and my feet were nearly burnt every day. Of course, with the blackout, we were not allowed lights, but one night the captain felt sorry for us and gave a bottle of gin to the chief wren. That was my first taste of alcohol. Each reunion, I meet ex– Superintendent Cole, and she always speaks of our days under canvas.

My next move was to St Andrews in Bristol, an old orphanage. We scrubbed and cleaned the place only to be told after a week that we were moving as it wasn't very suitable. We had rifle practice every day there.

Roseneath at Helensburgh on the Gareloch was next, looking after wrens and sailors in a Nissen hut encampment, with Americans, Canadians and British. There were about eight different camps there training on the landing craft for D Day. It was all very hush-hush, and our letters were all censored. To start work we had to have transport at 3 a.m. for a 3.30 start, then worked till 8; next day it was 8-4 pm, then 8-12 pm, then 8-8, four watches in rotation.

The food was cooked in several Nissen huts and dished up into mess tins for twelve to twenty people. Tea was put into a stockinette bag and dumped into a huge vat, bread slices counted out and butter and jam portioned. The bread was good because the camp had a bakery. If the sailors didn't return for lunch, their food was left until tea-time. It must have been horrible for them as there were no means of keeping the meal hot, except a rack above the long cooking stove. Men were practising with the landing craft for D Day and sometimes they didn't return.

I was made a Chief Wren and sent to Ardrossan Castle. The sailors were all in the big hall and it was my job to peep through the door to see they were all out of their hammocks in the morning so that the girls could go in and lay up the breakfasts for them. This place was full of steam flies – they seemed to accumulate in the pipes lagging. They were horrible, millions of them and in the evening I'd go round with a sailor with a blow torch to kill them. Quite a lot of places had these but nowadays they have modern chemicals to deal with them. I was still there in August 1945 when the war ended.

Food was dried mince, tinned stew, Australian rabbits in barrels and they were horrible, corned beef, pilchards, and tinned sausages, home made fish cakes and rissoles, dried egg which was alright if it was made properly, ship biscuits and always tinned milk. We made suet puddings, milk puddings and pastry. Cocoa was made with dark chocolate. Navy chocolate was hard and strong but they liked their night caps made with it. At teatime it was bread with jam, syrup, lemon curd or chocolate spread. Sometimes you got a pat of butter. No cakes of course. Suet puddings were called duff and they were made in huge containers. The kitchen was quite good but there were only eight baths there for thirty-two wrens.

One day, after being home for a weekend, I missed the ferry but the postman gave me a sail in his rowing boat across the Gareloch, and I was back in time.

We had a canteen at Clynder, near Rosneath, where we spent our off duty time. The sleeping quarters were in Nissen huts, six double-decker beds, six mats, a hanging fitment with a curtain for clothes and a bogey stove in the middle. From there I went to Dale Fort in South Wales, which was for degaussing wrens – that is, they were learning to use equipment to protect ships against magnetic mines. We only had paraffin stoves to cook on, but I was only there for a short time as I was rated a Petty Officer, and my next stop was at the signal station in Mumbles.

I looked after one male officer and twelve signal wrens. The officer had his early cup of tea and his radio on before seven o'clock, and I had to light the fire and have a little pan with just enough water in to make the tea. We did well for rations here because we were inside an American camp and we were given legs of pork etc, and large tins of fruit. For every ship that passed in and out of Swansea, the signal station was given money and I had a share.

Our social life was dancing at the Pier Hotel which let us in free. One night the wrens asked if they could stay out later and I told them they could creep in with me. We all had a good night. Coming home, I instructed them to follow me on tiptoe, but the Lieutenant was standing by his door, which we had to pass. After that, wrens had to sign-in in his room.

113

Levenmouth at War

I was very lucky to be not involved in any raids, perhaps because I was on the west coast all the time. When I went to Plymouth in 1946, the town had been flattened but I didn't see or hear anything of the war really. The only time was coming home on leave once we were stopped in the train because there was a raid on in Newcastle. The train stopped on a bridge.

When the war ended, I decided to stay on, progressing from Ordinary Wren, to leading Wren and Chief Wren, before coming back to Fife. If I had stayed another five years I might have been Fleet Chief, but I did twenty seven years altogether and was awarded the British Empire Medal in 1951.'

Janet's award ceremony

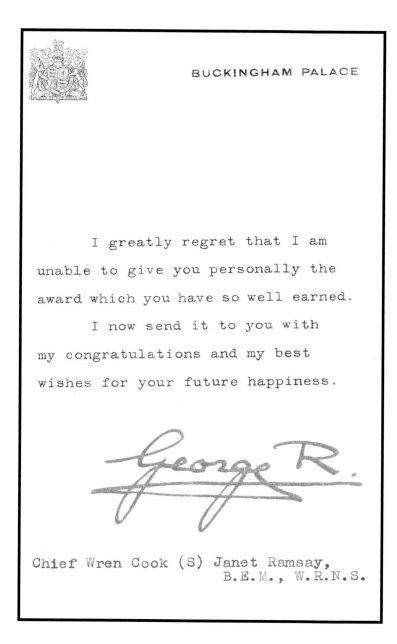

BUCKINGHAM PALACE

I greatly regret that I am unable to give you personally the award which you have so well earned.

I now send it to you with my congratulations and my best wishes for your future happiness.

George R.

Chief Wren Cook (S) Janet Ramsay,
B.E.M., W.R.N.S.

Levenmouth at War

AILEEN WHITE

Aileen White was born in Dundee but has spent most of her life in Fife. She vividly remembers the day war broke out.

'I was eight, and my Dad was called up about a week before the war started. He was in the Territorials and was one of the first to be away. He was in the Royal Signal Corps of the 51st Highland Division.

On that Sunday, we went to Kirkcaldy to my dad's parents. They'd made up their minds that since he was away, we should come and live with them. My uncle had a friend who ran a taxi business and he came to Dundee for us. My sister's cot was strapped to the roof. We stayed in Kirkcaldy for four months, with my mother nearly going crazy, in a two roomed house in March Street with an outside toilet. Mum, Isabel and I slept in a bed settee in the living room and Margo's cot was in my aunt's room with her little boy's bed. We went to Pathhead School and had to carry our gas masks everywhere. Grandfather varnished them to make them waterproof. I was astounded by the one for the baby, it was such a weird looking thing.

I was often bored at school so a favourite thing was the siren going off. Then we had to go down into the shelters and the teachers got us to sing. I didn't mind air raids during the night. It was an adventure. The shelter was in the garden with sandbags in front of it. Everything was ready to put on just in case the siren went and Mum had what she called her policy case with certificates and insurance policies in. We could hear the planes and knew the different sounds, watch the searchlights and listen to the adults talking. They made allowances at school the next day

Gas masks were tested every Friday. The teacher put a book under the mask and if it steamed up, it was working. The book stopped the air coming in. Our headmaster was head of the ATC before the war and he wore an officer's uniform.

Once we saw what he called a pickaback coming over the
Tay. It was a flying boat with a little plane on top.

Dad was captured in France. I saw him the first Christmas
after he went away because he was billeted in Kirkcaldy and
trained at Ravenscraig Park. He went to France in January or
February and was due home on leave in June but was captured
at St Valery where he won the Military Medal. He said very
little about it or about the prison camp, Stalag 383. Prisoners
were marched from France to Poland but he said he was
mostly in a lorry because his feet were so bad. The Germans
rode beside them in motorcycles and sidecars with machine
guns. Prisoners were fed on watery soup and if they stopped to
pick a potato out of a field, they would be shot. Then they
were packed in the holds of barges to be taken down the
Rhine.

They wouldn't have survived without the Red Cross. As
well as food parcels, they supplied musical instruments and
encouraged men to study, Dad passed exams for his work
while he was there. Mum collected for the Red Cross and
parcels had to be weighed. It was usually small things because
if you sent a jersey for instance, there wouldn't be enough
room for anything else. Cigarettes, of course; gloves, scarves,
pyjamas, soap, toothbrushes, combs small things that could be
traded . To help Red Cross funds, we made glitterwax flowers
with beech twigs and wax which could be softened and shaped
into flowers. We sold them at half a crown a bunch.

Towards the end of the war the Red Cross food parcels
didn't arrive. Dad was five foot ten and went down from
twelve and a half stone to six stones. They were liberated by
the Americans who immediately fed them, which was the
wrong thing to do, so when he came home Dad was in Bridge
of Earn Hospital for nine weeks.

He was released in June 1945 just after my fourteenth
birthday and Mum, Grandpa and I went to meet him at the
station. The train was late and there were hordes of men all
looking exhausted. They hadn't all been able to get seats and
travel was terrible at that time anyway. I'd gone forward a bit

to see if I could see him and this man ran to my mother and took her in his arms. He went right past me. He didn't know me . Mum said, 'Do you know who this is?' and he said 'No'.

I wouldn't have known him from Adam, he was so old compared to my mental picture of him – grey hair, not curly and dark and the face so different – he was a complete stranger. It was very difficult because we weren't accustomed to having a man in the house and it was strange. I was a big girl for my age, tall and mature and it would have been hard for him too, he wasn't used to women. After we went to bed, he came through and I remember him saying, 'Would you like me to kiss you goodnight?' I can weep yet thinking about it. He had kissed me at the station when we met, but he didn't know what was normal any more.

In some ways we resented him because he wanted a lot of Mum's company. She had just been living for the day when he'd come back. We weren't pushed into the background, but she used to talk to me about problems, money, Christmas presents and so on and suddenly I wasn't needed any more. The relationship took a long time to be natural, but actually I got on better with my father after I met my boyfriend. They were nothing like each other but Ron had been in the army – he went away the day the war finished – and had been in Germany so they had a lot in common. Ron was a draughtsman with Balfours and we began our married life in Methil.

The other thing that stands out for me was the scarcity of things and the queues. Mum would give us bus fares and two shillings to stand in a queue, once it was for three oranges and once for three delft mugs with no handles. Other queues were for combs, for a sponge at the baker's and I remember eating sour apples and lemons because you couldn't get fruit. At Christmas we'd gather shells from the beach, paint and thread them to make necklaces, and make felt flower brooches. We had make do and mend classes and one of our teachers had a suit made from two different patterned men's suits. It was hideous but she wore it all the time. We made blouses and skirts from men's shirts and trousers.

We listened to the radio a lot, programmes like Tommy Handley, Bebe Daniels and Ben Lyon; Dick Barton; The Palm Court Orchestra; Victor Sylvester; and lots of comedy shows and films – Laurel and Hardy and George Formby.'

Shipping gathering for convoy taking on crew and supplies

Levenmouth at War

JOSEPH MURRAY

Jo, one of five of a family, was born in 1932 and brought up at the Rosie. He spent his working life in the pit, beginning at the picking tables at the age of fourteen. Shortly afterwards he lost part of his foot because a safety shield had not been replaced. Joe's father was also a coal miner. He joined the Territorial Army to get a little extra money, but got rather more than he bargained for.

'Dad was in the Black watch and that was the first regiment to be called up. There was five of us and Johnny, the youngest was only months old. Dad was captured at Dunkirk. We were told he had bent down to give a wounded soldier a drink and a shell burst and shattered his knee.

He was in one of the Stalags and met up with a Mr Mitchell from Lochgelly. Mitchell wrote to his wife and asked her to come down and see that we were alright and we've been friends ever since. My Dad was in prison for five years and my Uncle Bobby took over the role of father to us and he and Auntie Lily helped look after us. My auntie who lived in the Highlands used to send us venison and salmon sometimes.

When he was freed by the Russians, Dad was working on a Polish farm. Johnny wouldn't believe it was our Dad when he came home.

The place was all done up with flags when the prisoners of war came home, and there were street parties, but my Dad wasn't well when he came home, and was never right after that. He went back to his job as a miner at the Rosie Pit.'

Levenmouth at War

DAVID DOWIE

David Dowie was born in Leven in 1918, and after leaving school, he started work as a porter in his father's auction business, before becoming a bricklaying apprentice first with Andrew Cook of Leven, and then with James Forrester and Son.

"On September 3rd 1939, my fiancée Margaret and I were singing our hearts out in the choir of St Michael's Church, Buckhaven, when the service was interrupted to inform us that we were now at war with Germany. I was called up for a medical which I failed, graded three, and to this day cannot understand why, because I was as fit as any fiddle. Around the turn of the year I was sent to Crail and helped build the aerodrome facilities, then worked on the Bridge of Earn Hospital buildings before building a wide range of workplaces - latrines, cook houses, in fact almost anything the army needed containing bricks and mortar.

My first real vision of war, apart from searchlight searches, was witnessing the Clydebank Blitz in March 1941, from a window in Alva, and hearing the drone of heavy bombers at times overhead as they headed to or from their targets..

I signed up in the home guard and took part in one exercise only. We were to meet in a local mansion house, in the middle of a wood somewhere. My duty, for the all night affair, was to guard a supposed crossing point away out in the country, and see to it that no one would pass. I was issued with a Sten gun, but no bullets. There was no moon, it was pitch black, and I got lost on the way back to base, where I was met by a cacophony of slumbering, snoring home guards. The exercise had been called off early but no one thought to tell me.

My next posting was Portmahomack in Ross-shire where workers were housed in Nissen huts. Our work place was the aerodrome at Fearn, close by Tain. When the building work on the flying field ended, I returned north again after a short visit home. We went by train to Scrabster, were shepherded on board the old *St Ola* steamer where we were battened down along with other animals, and we set sail. By the time we rounded the Old Man of Hoy, we had experienced the wrath of the converging Atlantic Ocean and the North Sea, and almost worse, the nauseating swell and roll of the waters approaching Stromness harbour. Our new home at Skeabrae was a jumble of about a dozen or so huts each accommodating about twenty four bodies, the same number of bunks and a rough storage cupboard, four long trestle type tables and a few stools.

Home comforts were non-existent, and in winter washing with cold water was not inviting, but looking back, we were remarkably content with our lot. Pastimes, important during the almost complete lack of daylight hours during the winter months, were essential. One problem was keeping warm. There are no trees on the Orkney mainland and, with howling gales, the resulting wind chill had to be experienced to understand. I stole a blanket and cut it up into bandage-like pieces and swathed myself from heel to chest in a reasonably effective underwear, though it was a bit itchy at times.

As both foreman and brick layers' union representative, I was able to cast my spell mainly from within a nice warm on site office, enjoying RAF tins of cigarettes, and the odd supply of coffee. I subsequently became the camp entertainment officer whose job it was to arrange ENSA visits and promote other functions in the cinema, including a visit by Gracie Fields and other dignitaries. I dealt with complaints about food problems, and had the camp cooks vary the menus within the limits of what was available to them, but was never quite successful in ridding the almost constant demands for mince and tatties

As work at the airfield dried up, and the need to maintain the station was no longer justified, I was transferred to a camp near Kirkwall, for a short time prior to the whole operation closing down. By early 1944, the need for further M.O.D. work had receded, but there was an urgent need for tradesmen skills to repair or rebuild the bomb-ravaged homes in the

English capital and elsewhere. Volunteers were called for to undertake this work on the understanding that they would be prepared to tackle any job, anywhere at the M.O.D's bidding. After a short break at home I headed south and arrived at Kingston-upon-Hull station complete with my old worthy tool. I knew that Hull had taken a severe battering in earlier years and thought that I would be fully occupied in rebuilding the place.

On arrival at the given address I was met by a friendly soul who explained to me that the materials and brushes had been delivered and I could start straight away. I was nonplussed to find that my job was to distemper the walls and ceilings in the house, with a choice of two colours, white and a yellowish brown. As day followed day performing similar functions, my expectations of an exciting worth-while rebuilding project gradually faded.

On the 15th or 16th of June 1944, I boarded a London bound train, was met at the station and driven from there to Aurelia Road in Croydon.

Our new base was flanked on three sides by domestic two storied buildings and on the other by a large brick built tramcar depot. Our accommodation consisted of the familiar Nissen huts. We were allocated bed space, that is a palliasse laid out on the hard floor, and all our worldly goods were packed into a sand bag, which then acted as a pillow. Not exactly The Ritz, but at the time there were no complaints. Toilet, kitchen and feeding facilities were pretty primitive.

We had no idea what we were doing here, so went for a walk. We had met and started a conversation with one of the locals when we were rudely interrupted and became aware of a strangely raucous and threatening rhythmic vibration, rapidly progressing in our direction. Then appeared over the rooftops what we took to be an aeroplane, but one of a kind that none of us had seen before and which seemed to be on fire. I turned round to ask the stranger for an explanation but he had disappeared. By this time the object had passed us by and was growling its way into the distance.

There was almighty explosion and a huge plume of black smoke appeared. Our erstwhile companion exited from a close by doorway and explained that this had been a new fangled pilot-less plane, which delivered a massive bomb to wherever it landed. Once heard, the V1 jet propulsion system's roar would forever be recognised for what it was, and still, sixty years on, when television documentaries or such like replay the past, the hair on the back of my neck reacts, and memories, good and bad, return.

Later on that same evening I experienced my first doodlebug foray, and decided that taking refuge in the tram shed offered a safer haven than a Nissen hut. However, it was only then that I discovered that the shed had been converted into the local mortuary. Some time later I booked a bunk in a nearby shelter situated at the entrance to the Mitcham road cemetery. This move was to play an essential part in my survival later on.

Doodlebugs took a heavy toll on the citizens and infrastructure in the Croydon area, and elsewhere. Being in the direct line of fire between the launch sites in France and London, Croydon received a high percentage of hits, and hospitals, children's homes and similar institutions were not immune from the one-ton payloads.

I restored weather proofing to badly damaged roofs, blown out frontages, glass-less windows, etc. using whatever materials came to band.

As one could first hear and then see the V1's approaching everyone more or less hit the ground until the weapon continued on its way or suddenly dipped and exploded. Then tactics changed, the power would cut out quite a long way from the destination but, from moving at around four hundred miles an hours, the lifeless plane continued on its way for many miles before losing all momentum and becoming a noiseless threat akin to a falling leaf, and this was scary. Not too bad if the skies were clear and there was always the chance of seeing the thing, but dull days were dreaded, no sight, no sound, just *bang*. One day I was repairing a roof, when I became aware of a bomb coming down a few hundred yards away. I don't recall how I got down the roof ladder but had a hard landing just seconds before the missile buried itself in an adjacent open field. The roof I had been working on was now in much more need of repair than before.

In retrospect, there were some instances of the funny side, though not at the time, when things nearly went wrong. Picture Dowie walking along the ridge of a two-storey building and about to replace roof and ridge tiles previously damaged. A thirty foot roof ladder with an appropriate holding pin was in place and Jamie, one of my mates, was perched on it. A doodlebug was spotted heading directly towards me. I scrambled onto the roof ladder and the pin gave way. By some miracle I managed to stop my downward slide grabbing what was left of the ridge, but Jamie was left hanging on to the ladder about a couple of feet from, and swinging free of the building. We made it to safety somehow, but to rub salt into the wound, the doodlebug passed safely overhead into the far distance.

In the early morning of 3rd August 1944, I was rudely awakened and instinctively knew that the campsite had been hit. I hurriedly arose and ran round to be met with a scene of absolute devastation, death and destruction and found myself in a state of shock. During that fateful forenoon, together with survivors, I wandered around the wreckage, retrieving what we could of the personal belongings of the dead and the living.

Those were handed over to Wardens and other officials who arrived on the scene, and in a pool of blood and on the spot where I would have been sleeping had I not moved, I collected my bricklayer's trowel. I still have it, lying rusting in the garage.

By midday, all that we could do had been done, the eleven dead now laid out in the remains of the mortuary. All my bits and pieces found were put into a Hessian sand bag, I was given a train ticket pass, some cash and told to entrain for Buckhaven and await further instructions. At the entrance to the station there was a kiosk, and of all things in war time there was displayed a bunch of black grapes. I asked the attendant if I could have them and was told rather haughtily that they would cost me five shillings, a lot of money then. Anyway I bought them and, carried in a paper bag, they were handed over to a very surprised Margaret the following morning. I had neither washed nor eaten since supper two days before but clean or dirty, I was home.

A week later I found myself retracing my journey, but this time my billet had no fear of flying bombs. I spent the rest of my time playing a piano or games in the depths of the reinforced concrete of Epsom racecourse stand. I was a first floor occupant, just about where Her Majesty appears on race days, and was ideally placed to observe in safety the VI s heading for the winning post from the direction of Tottenham comer.

By this time the doodlebug menace was vastly reduced as their launching pads were over-run by the Allies and the defences on this side were much improved. However it became clear that another much more sinister weapon was being deployed, the rocket propelled V2. Although it was more destructive than the VI, being timed to explode underground, it did not hold the same terror. Whereas the flying menace was heard, seen and feared, the V2 did not have the same effect because, travelling faster than sound, you either heard the explosion or you didn't. I spent my last working days based down south at Epsom until, in early November I received a letter requesting me to return home as father had been taken ill and was in hospital where a consultant wished to see me. My father had cancer, he died in April 1945 and I took over his business as an auctioneer. But that, as they say, is another story.'

Levenmouth at War

KEN MCEWEN

'I lived with my parents in a semi-detached house overlooking the harbour at Crail, with sweeping views over the entrance to the Firth together with quite a long stretch of the Southern side.

I had a wonderful view from the attic window and put my powerful three-draw telescope to good use. One unforgettable pre-war sight was the pale grey HMS *Hood* building up speed as she headed out into the North Sea with a "bone in her bough" and a "roosters tail" at the stern. Magnificent, but sadly never seen again.

We heard the Prime Minister's speech to the nation, which was followed by an air raid siren. We all went outside, but saw nothing, heard nothing so went back inside.

Black out screens and curtains were put up and the effectiveness checked by the local constable who left big footprints in Mum's flower garden.

I had just turned fifteen in July, had just learned to use a shot-gun on a friend's farm and could get a couple of rabbits from time to time, and fished occasionally, so food was not a problem.

When construction of an aerodrome got under way between Crail and Fife Ness, my cousin Dave came to board with us together with some of his mates. Home life became more lively and I had some male company.

My usual transport to school was the daily Bluebird bus or by bicycle. School fire drills were modified and enlarged upon to become air raid drills, and gas masks in cardboard boxes were supposed to be carried everywhere, but that didn't last long.

The air raid policy was dispersal. No groups were to be formed, exit points were defined and the rule was that everyone had to be undercover within five minutes. No air-raid shelters were built, and local pupils took out of towners with them when they ran home. In my case, a classmate from

Elie accompanied me in a mini "cross-country" as we galloped over the fields and across the Dreel Burn en route to Grannie's house in Shore Road.

The first casualty among Waid former pupils was David Pryde, a fighter pilot and son of the Kilrenny minister. He was given a RAF funeral at a cemetery near the school, with a firing party, and three Gladiator fighters flying in salute above the cemetery. The school was well represented and it was very impressive.

Even before September 3rd, reservists had been called up from local fishing fleets and there was a marked increase in naval movements in the Firth with manoeuvring and firing exercises being carried out.

In October, we experienced our first air raid of any significance when a group of Junkers 88 bombers flew up the Firth to attack naval units in retaliation for an RAF raid on Willemshaven. It came after lunch on Oct 16th. We were in Bill Ferrier's English class on the top floor of Waid. It was a warm day and the windows were partially open. We heard sounds of distant gun-fire and, as it became louder, we jumped up and opened the windows wide. Bill Ferrier was furious. 'Sit down boys. Its just a practice,' he said.

There had been no warning. We were just in time to see columns of water from a few bombs which fell near an escorted convoy, and very short glimpses of aircraft in breaks in the cloud. It was all over very quickly, a few more bangs and bumps in the distance, then silence.

My first memory is of the speed of modern air warfare. It was the first time we had heard the noise of eight guns on a Spitfire firing in unison and the best description of the sound was that it was similar to ripping calico. All the boys were surprised by the speed of it all.

We had been nurtured on the excitement of Biggles and the Red Baron chasing each other's tails, with white silk scarves streaming behind. A year after this raid I was at home on a non-school day, a Saturday I think, because Mum had done a washing and I was sitting on the front step swotting.

Suddenly, a Heinkel III bomber came out of cloud and seemed to be heading straight for me.It dropped a short stick of four bombs. The first exploded on the rocks below our house the second hit the corner of a house in Temple Park Crescent, injuring one of the elderly lady occupants, and the others fell in open country beyond the Police station.

On hearing the first explosion, I hurled myself along the front passage and arrived under the staircase in time to knock Dad's legs from under him as he emerged from the bathroom. At the rear of the house, Mum had been hanging out the washing and on the way in she stopped for a chat over the hedge with our next-door neighbour, Mrs Duncan. They looked up at the approaching plane and Mum said "Look, there's a man falling from it." I'm glad to say that these were not Mother's last words.

I remember one more air raid incident at about the same time. I was visiting my pal Bill Chapman after school and we were sitting on the back lawn when a Dormer D.O. 17 , known as the *Flying Pencil*, flew immediately above us and fairly low down. It was pursued by two Hurricane fighters on full boost with black smoke coming from their exhausts.

Bombs were unloaded on the new Fleet Air Arm aerodrome, but the results were unknown.

A branch of the Air Training Corps had been formed at the Waid, and I joined. We learned the basics of signalling, i.e. Morse Code by key and lamp; flag semaphore; marching drills; aircraft recognition ; navigation ; cloud formations, etc.

It was a thrill for me to be invited to a camp on the aerodrome for a whole week early in 1941. We were on the temporary establishment of H.M.S. *Jackdaw,* and we were hosted, fed, and drilled by the Petty Officers.

We were given talks by pilots returning from operations and acting as instructors for trainee pilots of torpedo bombers such as *Swordfish* and *Albacore*. We sat in the cockpits and learned the instrumentation, saw aircraft guns being calibrated and ranged at the firing butts, and were even allowed to briefly press the trigger on a tripod mounted machine gun. It was all very exciting and one of the shortest weeks I have ever experienced.

On another occasion we were taken out to a ship in the Forth which was acting as a target-ship for a torpedo dropping aircraft. We observed several attacks, had them explained to us, then ate sandwiches, tomatoes and Carnation tinned milk. Some were sick, but it was a great day.

My best pal Bill was ahead of me at Waid and broke off his business training course in Glasgow to volunteer for fighters pilot training in the Fleet Air Arm.

I left school in 1941 to take up a Drafting Cadetship in London, where I lived with my sister and her husband and shortly after this Dad and Mum sold up at Crail and moved to London to once again be closer as a family.

The last link with Crail was broken. Bill was killed in a flying accident and this prompted me to join the RAF in 1942, opening up a new chapter in my life.'

HMS Rodney and destroyers in the Firth of Forth

Levenmouth at War

JANET THOMSON

Janet Thomson came to Buckhaven when her family bought a business there but she was brought up in Falkirk. At the age of fourteen, she was working twelve hours a day in a tobacconist shop for eight shillings a week.

'When I was called up, I was given the choice of going into one of the services, but my friend was not old enough to be called up so she asked me to wait and go with her when she got her papers. But I was in munitions by then and they wouldn't allow me to leave, so she went into another factory.

We worked two shifts, day and night shift. I had to go in earlier at night because the tool setters had to set up the machines for the girls to work. Sometimes you would be working for hours on one machine and couldn't get it right. The machines had to be dead on because the girls were on piece work and the more bombs they put out, the more money they got. We made bombs about twelve to fourteen inches long. They were really heavy.

I didn't have much training, I worked on the machines for about three weeks and at that time the shell factory which had not long opened, had men tool setters and seven or eight of us on the machines. One of my friends was made a tool setter and the boss thought I was good enough to train. At that time, all we were thinking about was the money. The first week I got five pounds in my hand and I thought it was a fortune. It was very interesting and I did love my job. On night shift I began at eight and the girls at nine, and we worked till seven thirty in the morning, with two breaks for tea or coffee.

We were making the hole at the top of the bomb case to put the explosive in and we had a device to test the size of the hole. It had to be exactly right, dead on. We had labourers coming in during the night with barrows, which they loaded with bombs to take them away to be filled at another place. We didn't have explosives in our factory, we were all inexperienced workers and we had good times and rotten times. Our factory closed down and I was sent to another. I hated it and started getting jittery, I'd been on it far too long, about four years, so I got laid off and then was excused more war work

We didn't have raids in Falkirk but we were quite close to the aerodrome at Grangemouth, and we'd watch the planes coming over. We saw the Clydebank bombing, the whole sky a mass of raging flames and that was twenty five miles away.'

Soldiers and ATS ; dispatch rider on motorcycle
Etta Gullen Barrie St. second left

LIEUTENANT COLONEL WIESLAW SZCZYGIEL

GEORGE HARVEY

George Harvey was born Wieslaw Szczygiel *in Poland in 1919. He became a regular army officer of the 1st Polish Parachute Brigade, took part in the battle of Arnhem and later served as Staff Officer of the Headquarters of The Polish Resettlement Corps. Demobbed in 1948, he started a photographic business in Leven and Kirkcaldy. He retired in 1996.*

'In September 1939 Hitler's army invaded Poland under the pretext of gaining the free city of Gdansk and creating a so-called corridor between Germany and East Prussia. Although Poland had a comparatively large army, and small air force, we were not equipped sufficiently to match the technically superior German forces. Our defensive campaign of some three weeks might have lasted longer if Poland had not been invaded by her eastern neighbour, the Soviet Union.

Since most of the Polish forces were withdrawing eastwards under German pressure, many units as well as some civilians escaped to the then neutral Romania, Hungary and the Baltic States. Eventually, they found their way to France where a Polish Army was being formed by the Polish Government in Exile, led by General Sikorski.

By May 1940, three Polish Army divisions were involved in the French defence against Germany. One was defeated on the front line, another was interned in Switzerland and, after Dunkirk and the fall of France on 17th June, the remnants of the Third Division retreated to the West of France from where they were evacuated to the UK.

Many of the soldiers of these units were Polish emigrants to France and Belgium who settled there before the war and decided to stay there in spite of the German occupation. This resulted in the units arriving in the UK having a disproportionately large number of officers and officer cadets who had originally escaped from Poland. In July 1940 there were twenty six thousand Polish troops in the UK. Of these, four thousand officers and twelve and a half thousand men were in the Army, the rest in the Polish Air Force and Navy. All of the Army units were transferred to Scotland and some of them were posted in Fife.

The 1st Rifle Brigade was given the task of defending North-East Fife, so Brigade H.Q. and 2nd Battalion was stationed in Cupar and Ladybank, the 3rd Battalion in St. Andrews and the 1st in the camp at Tentsmuir. Other units were in Newport and Tayport. The troops were billeted mostly in church, community, Masonic halls and empty hotels. The Battalion in Tentsmuir camp was accommodated in Nissen Huts built there by a Polish Army Engineers Company of which I was a member for some time. The Nissen huts were nick-named 'Barrels of Laughter,' but it was no laugh as they were too hot in the summer and freezing cold in the winter with only one iron stove to give local heat.

The battalion was there before the camp was quite finished and I remember a dreich October day when, in pouring rain, the Battalion was lined up. A group of high-ranking Polish officers in their square hats with equally high-ranking British officers accompanied a portly civilian in a raincoat and a peculiar black hat. I later learned that it was Mr. Churchill himself inspecting the newly arrived defenders of the United Kingdom. Those defenders were thinly spread and poorly equipped. Although the French rifles were replaced by slightly less antiquated British models from the First World War, there were few machine guns and even fewer artillery pieces.

Our main task was to defend Fife from a possible German air and sea invasion, which, if successful, could have cut off north-east Scotland from the South. The defensive concrete positions and beach obstacles were there when we arrived and were later supplemented. Our fire power was limited to rifles, light machine guns, a few mortars and a limited number of artillery pieces and Bren gun carriers. The Home Guard, with which we were collaborating, was also poorly armed.

When the threat of the German invasion passed, most of the Polish army units were reorganised, and one of those was the 4th Cadre Rifle Brigade. It was given the sector from Anstruther to Buckhaven which was far too large an area for a unit which was effectively a battalion, consisting mainly of officers. The idea was to form later a full-strength unit from Polish volunteers from other parts of the world. The total strength of this unit on arrival in Fife was some four hundred officers and just over a hundred other ranks.

The Cadre Brigade was established as a battalion of three infantry companies, an artillery unit and nuclei of other units like sappers, signals etc. Initially the units were stationed in Lundin Links, Largo, and Elie with their headquarters and some services in Leven. We were billeted in hotels and boarding houses which were plentiful in these holiday localities but empty because of the war. Some officers were billeted with local families.

The Brigade arrived in Fife in October 1940. Our units had the task of manning the existing defence positions, preparing others to accommodate the few light machine guns and patrolling the shoreline. During the monotony of our manning the defences and patrolling the beaches we had the chance to appreciate the terrific effort the British made in a comparatively short time since the outbreak of hostilities in the preparation of shore and inland defences. There were miles of anti-tank blocks and minefields, concrete bunkers and anti-landing obstacles, in the form of tall telegraph poles imbedded in concrete on the beaches. The remains of some of these defences are still here today.

This period was also the opportunity for closer contact between ourselves and our hosts, and. get to know each other. Our initial impressions of the Scottish friendly attitude and their hospitality was soon confirmed. In spite of our lack of knowledge of the language, there were friendly invitations to local homes or cordial encounters with the male population in local bars when many a time a Polish soldier was treated all evening by the locals. This male, friendly attitude mellowed with time when the Scots discovered the Poles' great popularity among the local female population, who were not averse to the Polish continental charm, politeness, generosity and smart appearance.

Romances blossomed, developing in time into marriages which however were not encouraged by the army authorities. For instance, our brigadier had a rule that any officer's or soldier's application for permission to marry had to lie on his commanding officer's desk for six weeks before it was submitted to the Brigadier. This was in the hope that the applicant might change his mind during the six weeks. Nonetheless many friendships lasted till the end of the war and ended in happy marriages.

During our first year there were all sorts of training courses, including English language classes. In each locality there was usually a canteen run by the local ladies of the Red Cross, WVS or FANY, providing some literature, a friendly chat over a cup of tea and buns and a language lesson. Parties and dances were organised in local halls with Polish army bands playing the popular sentimental tunes. Soon they picked up the Scottish tunes and dances. Language was no barrier even when a Polish bandmaster invited all to 'Strip The Widow.'

Many of the officers of all ages and ranks were regular army officers but the majority were army reserve junior officers mobilised in 1939 who escaped the German and Soviet occupation to avoid their policy of destroying Poland's educated classes. There were university students, teachers, doctors, engineers, civil servants and other professionals in ages ranging from their twenties to their fifties.

For those older ones especially it was difficult to adapt to the strange country, language and customs where men wore skirts, drank tea with milk and spoiled their good whisky by adding water or worse still lemonade. We also had to adapt to local customs and army drill. The British monetary system took some time to get used to. After being brought up on the decimal system, twelve pence in a shilling and twenty shillings in the pound seemed strange. The same applied to imperial weights and measures. Map reading took some time to get used to.

The new arrivals retained most of their customs and original forms of behaviour, which often seemed strange but not necessarily unwelcome by the natives. They still shook hands at every meeting, bowed, clicked their heels and kissed ladies' hands. They dressed smartly, some used after-shave lotion and carried dispatch cases. The officers' square hats were regarded as a curiosity, although the majority of officers did not have them, and those who did wore them on formal occasions only. Polish soldiers, singing their songs as they marched, were also an innovation in war-time Scotland.

Our Colonel Sosabowski was a man of action and a strict disciplinarian. Not satisfied with the fairly passive role of his Brigade, he started to organise a unit which could be used eventually in the liberation of Poland. Colonel, later Major General, Sosabowski was a hard man, not only to the men under his command but also to himself. At the age of fifty four he underwent the complete parachute training and jumped in the battle of Arnhem.

He was feared but respected and even liked by his subordinates who recognised his devotion to the cause and his concern for the welfare of his men. He ruffled a few feathers both in the Polish and British high circles and received no thanks for it. His greatness was recognised in present-day Poland where a Polish Parachute Brigade bears his name and his monument stands in the barracks square in Krakow.

In 1941, our officers were sent in strict secrecy on courses already being run by the British authorities preparing personnel for underground work in occupied Europe. One of the means of placing these underground workers in the enemy-occupied countries was by parachute. This was how our Parachute Brigade started its existence. Our volunteers went to the British Parachute Training School run by the Air Force at Ringway Airport near Manchester

As the number of prospective trainees grew, an idea of preliminary parachute training emerged and so Largo House with its extensive grounds became the training centre. The main part of training was intensive physical exercises with the use of equipment which prepared volunteers for jumping and landing in combat conditions. All the equipment had to be invented, improvised and constructed by the officers and men of the Brigade, and included an imitation plane fuselage. All sorts of swings, trapezes and other obstacles were constructed among the old buildings and trees surrounding Largo House and it soon gained the nick-name of 'Monkey Grove.' In time a parachute jumping tower designed by a Polish Army engineer was constructed at Lundin Links. It was later copied by the British Airborne Forces.

As the reorganisation of the Polish Army in Scotland progressed, our Brigade started receiving volunteers from other units and a part of the 2nd Rifle Battalion stationed in Cupar was para-trained in Largo House and Ringway. In Largo House there were also French, Norwegian and Czech officers trained as paratroopers to be dropped for underground work in their countries, and over three hundred Polish underground workers were trained there over the years and parachuted into occupied Poland.

By September 1941 we had nearly four hundred trained parachutists and so, to receive the recognition and approval of the Polish and British authorities, an exercise with the use of aircraft from the British Para School in Ringway was organised and executed on the exercise fields of Kincraig near Elie. It was a historical day not only for us but also for Scotland, first in history a mass drop of a company of paratroopers on Scottish soil.

The news of the planned exercise spread and the hills surrounding the dropping zone were crowded by the locals. On a prominent point was a gathering of high-ranking British and Polish officers led by the Polish Prime Minister, General Sikorski.

The scheme to simulate the attack on the coastal artillery battery on Kincraig Point went according to plan and without casualties. After the exercise General Sikorski in his speech announced "From today you are the 1st Polish Independent Parachute Brigade."

From this date the Brigade had an official standing as a para-brigade with the task of being eventually used in the liberation of Poland, so the Brigade's motto *By the Shortest Way*, was coined.

There were other momentous days in the Brigade's history. One was in September 1943 when Lady Victoria Wemyss presented the Brigade with a handsome banner from the ladies of Fife. Another gift was the regimental standard presented by the 1st British Airborne division as a fraternal token. The most important event was in June 1944 when on the fields of Cupar the Polish President presented the Brigade the Regimental Colours produced in Occupied Poland and smuggled out from there. Under these banners we went to the battle at Arnhem.

Other important occasions were when our intensive training was sometimes inspected by the high-ranking Polish and British dignitaries. And so, we had the visit of the Deputy Prime Minister, Clement Atlee, the Polish President and numerous British and Polish Generals.

The strength of the Brigade was at first supplemented by volunteers from units stationed in Scotland, and later by Polish nationals who were conscripted into the German Army and surrendered to the Allies at the defeat of Rommel in North Africa. The largest number of reinforcements came, however, from the Polish Army being formed in the Middle East after evacuation from Soviet Russia. Those volunteers were mostly young but without military training and in poor physical condition after the privations of two years in Soviet prisons. Proper nutrition and intensive physical training soon made them good soldiers.

By 1944 our total strength was three thousand but some units were under strength. Our equipment and uniforms were standard British Army, the only difference from the British

Army uniforms being grey berets instead of red, shoulder flashes with "POLAND" on them, rank insignia and collar badges of a parachute on a grey background with yellow piping.

By the summer of 1944 the Brigade was almost ready to be used in action. The British authorities were determined to use the Brigade in the liberation of Europe but for political and technical reasons not in the Warsaw Rising although this had been our intention from the start. In June, the Brigade was posted to East England for final training and readiness for a drop into the Continent. This took place in September 1944, not as expected in Poland, but at Arnhem. This is another story which has been described at length elsewhere.

After Arnhem, the Brigade was evacuated to England where it was reorganised, reinforced and posted to Germany as part of B.A O.R. In Fife remained some non-combat units, consisting mainly of officers and men who, for age and health reasons were not fit for active service. There also remained other units in Kirkcaldy, Dunfermline, Cowdenbeath and other Fife towns.

When war ended, the Poles had an option of either returning to Poland under the Communist domination, emigrating to other countries or joining the Polish Resettlement Corps to be trained for civilian occupations and settling in the UK. Many did so, although prospects of employment were limited. Those with family ties soon settled, found some jobs or started their own businesses and improved their English, or should I say Scots, as many acquired a good Fife accent.

And here we still are, the remnants of the Polish arrivals of 1940, leaving some visible signs of the Polish troops who were stationed in Fife. There are still a few permanent relics like the mosaic on the wall of the Town Hall in St. Andrews, the nameplate marking the Polish Camp Road in Tentsmuir Forest, a plaque on the wall of Earlsferry Town Hall, the icon of Holy Mary in the Royal Chapel in Falkland Palace, and, erected after the War, the monument of General Sikorski in, St

Levenmouth at War

Andrews, the monument of Scottish - Polish friendship in Leven and, more recently, the Polish Forces Museum which Fife Council has taken under its care.'

Concrete defence blocks at Leven

MARY BELL

'I tried to join the Wrens in 1939 when I was seventeen, I wanted to go before I was called up. My father was an ex-RSM in the Black Watch and I was working on a farm, which was going to convert to Land Army girls and I didn't fancy that. I'd done a season at the lambing that winter, out at all hours and I wasn't keen on that either, so I went to the Caird Hall in Dundee. They said I was too young, but in May when I was eighteen I applied for the Wrens. I had to get three references, from a doctor, a minister and someone who was in the services. Luckily my uncle was a commander in the navy and I managed to get hold of him.

I had to report to Dundee for my medical and started off at *Ambrose*, which was the teacher training college at Dundee. I trained for a year in general duties because I found that they covered a multitude of sins. I didn't have the intelligence for radio or things like that but I passed out as a Leading Hand and was sent to HMS *Jackdaw* at Crail. I was a stewardess for six months at Crail House then was transferred to the hospital in Crail village. Being brought up in the country, in a small community, going into the forces was a difficult experience and it was difficult to make friends at first, but I really enjoyed it.

They asked for volunteers for London and I went down for a fortnight relieving some girls to let them get a rest from the bombing. Stationed at Twickenham we used to come into Greenwich and there were heavy raids. It was pretty grim and noisy and once the billet I was in was hit. We were in the shelter that night and woke up in the morning to see the gable end of the house had disappeared. I didn't like travelling through London with all the buildings at the stage of collapsing, but we got used to it. I was at HMS *Jackdaw* at Crail for three years with spells in London.

They asked for volunteers again and I went to Portsmouth and was there till 1945. The worst of the bombing was over before I went there but the doodlebugs were worse. I was transferred to the Royal Marines for a time in Kent and where we were was known as Doodlebug Alley. They sounded like an old motor bike chugging along, but when they stopped you took shelter or hoped you weren't too near. Once, going back to Sussex, I went to the Union Jack Club for breakfast after getting off the overnight train. We heard the bomb but didn't pay much attention. It landed at the back of Kings Cross Station and we had to dive under the table for cover. There were sausages flying all over the place.

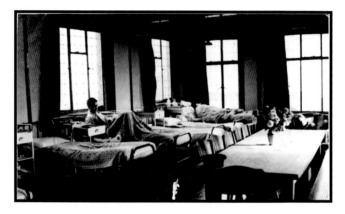

Hospital ward at HMS Jackdaw

I was promoted to Leading Hand before I went to Crail but lost my stripe once. The first time, I was home on leave and didn't get back in time because we were held up by a road accident. The second time, I should never have been on leave because the invasion was on, we couldn't get home and were fed up. The girl I shared a cabin with invited me to her home and got me a pass. On the way back the train was stopped because of doodlebugs and we had to get in to buses and didn't get back till four in the morning.

We were meant to be due back at eight in the evening so I was up in front of the Captain with a great crowd of men who were defaulters. I got my stripe back eventually and stayed on as a Leading Hand. I could have gone on to be a Petty Officer but I felt that was too much. I had enough responsibility and didn't want more. Besides, when you joined the officer class, you lost all your friends.

I moved from general dogsbody to sick bay steward to officers steward and when I left Ford I was in charge of a mess because it was what was called a kicking-off place . Men were coming in for demobilisation and my job was pretty hectic. It was Fleet Air Arm there and you'd get word in the morning that about two hundred men were coming in to go on draft. You had to make sandwiches and lunch boxes for all of them, but I had a good team.

When we were off duty in Crail, we'd walk along the beach to the canteen at Anstruther. At the bigger stations, we had ENSA, dances and so on. You had to go on courses and once we went up to Edzell and had to live out in the wild on our own. The weather wasn't too bad, we had some food but had to find the rest. I remember we took bits of someone's drystone dyke to make an oven. It was good fun and you learned to live as a team.

Not everyone managed; some people went home on leave and didn't come back but of course they got punished. I went to sea a couple of times – across the channel to the Isle of Wight. We went out to ships but never served on them. In Dundee we had a good time because the troops from Poland came to Dundee when Hitler invaded them. In our mess room, we had King Haakon of Norway, and Prince and Princess Bernard of the Netherlands. Their yacht was lying in the Tay.

The Prince was an officer in the Royal navy and they lived on the yacht for a time. There was a party on board and at that time, everything was getting very scarce but the meal we got and the pastries were out of this world. The week King Haakon was there, the Norwegians went to town and we went on duty in the morning to find they'd used our eggs to plaster the walls. We had stewards from their ship working in our Mess, and between the language difficulties and the bad temper, there were sparks flying many a time.

I met General de Gaulle when he was giving honours to sailors on the Catalina flying boats. The Free French were there and we weren't supposed to be but we went up on to the roof and watched. I didn't like being back in Civvy Street, and found it difficult to settle. I'd got married during the war to a Canadian who was with the Eighth Army at Cassino and was killed just before Christmas, 1944. I wanted to go out to Canada with the other war brides but I let my father put his foot down. That was a mistake and I never met my husband's family. I married again four years later, this time to a Fifer.

Wartime life had to be lived from day to day, just trusting that your number didn't come up. That's what kept the Londoners going, I think. Houses were dropping in the street, firemen rescuing people but others went about their business as usual. You'd get friendly with people, ships would sail and next thing you'd hear, they'd been blown up. My second husband was torpedoed twice. Ships coming back from Charleston bringing Monty and Churchill back to Britain without a full escort were bombed in the Mediterranean. He had to take half a ship back to Charlestown and was bombed and torpedoed again but all the crew managed to escape.'

Nurses and patients at HMS Jackdaw

JIMMY LAIRD

Jimmy Laird, who was twelve and lived in Adamson Terrace, recalled being in the Foreman Church in Leven the day that war broke out.

'I can always remember I was sitting in the kirk with my Granny and my Mother and the minister announced we were at war. A few minutes after that, he said there was an air raid warning in progress, and he advised us all to go home. It was strange to me. I didn't think a lot about it as I wasn't paying much attention to what the minister was saying and then some of the older women started greeting. We came out of the Kirk and the first thing I saw was an air raid warden with a steel helmet, he was on his bike, blowing a whistle and cycling up and down the road. There was supposed to be an air raid going on but nothing came near us, nothing happened.

I became an ARP indoor messenger in December 1942 when I left school and started at the steel works, The National Steel Foundry at Kirkland where they were making casts for bombs and things like that. My job was in the core shop oiling the cores that the girls made. Those were the moulds they made to pour the molten metal into. We had to oil them so they wouldn't fall apart, then they were baked in an oven. That was my first job, it maybe lasted about a year, then I went to Balfours in Leven to serve my apprenticeship as a plater there.

It was during the time I was in the steelworks I joined the ARP messenger service. I can always remember the first time the air raid siren sounded during the night. We were all sitting coorying under the stairs. There was my mother, my two sisters and my twin brothers who were born two months after the war started and I remember the gas mask hoods, we had to put the whole bairn inside it and pump the bellows. After a few times one got used to the sirens and didn't even bother to get out of bed. When I started as an ARP messenger I had to get up and go down to the White Memorial Centre in Leven, which was down where Nicol's golf club works used to be. I was too young to be allowed out on a bike so I had to be inside the building, carrying messages from one room to another about where the raiders were supposed to be and so on. That was the ARP headquarters for the Wemyss area. They didn't have so many intercoms or telephones in those days and I was only a very small cog in the wheel. Being in a reserved occupation, I missed being conscripted in 1945 but was called up in 1946, and did my National Service in The Black Watch with the B.A.O.R. in Germany.

I can mind the early days of the Home Guard. They started off as the Local Defence Volunteers or LDV, which people said stood for 'Look, Duck and Vanish.' They just wore armbands in those early days. I started off with the Home Guard Cadets, which later became the Army cadets and served for a lot of years after I came back from National Service and was eventually commissioned in 1954.

I remember once that bombs were dropped on fields near Balgrummo Farm up the road a bit, I think it was four bombs that dropped in total. The sirens sounded after the bombs fell. The next day we were up there looking for bits of shrapnel. That was the nearest raids we had. I remember often hearing the bombers going across, with their distinctive sound. Where I lived in Adamson Terrace you could look down into the Forth and see the ships out there. We knew when a raid was due because the ships would get what was called a yellow warning and the barrage balloons would go up to stop the low level bombing. The red message was when the sirens were sounded.

My dad was in France in the first world war and joined the Territorials after that. He was a Sergeant Major in the Black Watch. T.A. and when the second war was imminent and conscription started, they asked for volunteers to join the regular army as Sergeant instructors. My dad was one of the volunteers. He was on a course at Dover Castle when the war started. When he went back to Perth he used to come home every other weekend and help train the Home Guard. We were brought up quite regimental. At one time there were four of us in uniform when my brothers joined the cadets and there was nothing but khaki and blancoing belts and so on for parades at the weekend.

After a time at Queens Barracks in Perth my dad was posted to St Andrews University to train the Officers Training Corps there till he retired. He was a soldier all his life When you look back on the war years, some things stand out. There was always a sense of excitement, a change from day to day life. I remember the Polish troops coming into Leven Station and we learned some of the Polish words. Leven became full of Polish troops and they were billeted in the Masonic Hall and other venues around the town.

Not long before that I remember the Black Watch Territorials marching down Station Road getting ready to go away to France, with their pipers in front, and all the women on the platform saying their farewells. The Royal Artillery Territorials (Leven Battery) left at a separate time.

We were lucky not to have more air raids here because of the convoys out in the Forth and the importance of Methil Docks as a port with ships being loaded up and ready to move out.

I got my defence medal for my ARP service. I remember climbing out of the attic window on VE day to put the flag up on the roof and I had a couple of thunder flashes from my cadet days and I set them off. The neighbours must have thought the war had started again.'

COLONEL SIR JOHN EDWARD GILMOUR, DSO, TD, JP.

The Gilmour family have been in Montrave since about 1860, when the family returned to Scotland from Canada where they were shipbuilders. The present baronet, Sir John Gilmour lived in the house from August to January every year from 1920 till the war. His father was a Member of Parliament, so the family and household stayed in London from January to the end of July. First elected to the House of Commons in 1910 as Conservative member for East Renfrewshire, Sir John, senior, had since 1918, represented the Pollok Division of Glasgow.

He was Secretary of State for Scotland from 1932 – 1935, and just before the war' was Lord High Commissioner for the General Assembly, a position his son held later, and lived at Holyrood Palace while carrying out his Commissioner's duties. Neville Chamberlain came and stayed, and Alec Douglas Hume was his parliamentary private secretary. A distinguished soldier and statesman, Sir John commanded the Fife and Forfar Imperial Yeomanry during the First World War, and was appointed Minister for Shipping in 1940.

The present baronet, Sir John Gilmour, joined the Fife & Forfar Yeomanry in 1931, the year he left Eton and was commissioned in April 1932. The Regiment was recruited, one squadron in Dunfermline, one in Kirkcaldy, one in Cupar/St Andrews and one in Forfar. When the Territorial army was doubled in the summer of 1938, they went to camp in 1939 as two regiments and Sir John became squadron leader of the Dunfermline squadron in the second regiment.

'There were two regiments. The first went to France in 1940 and eventually came out through Dunkirk and lost their commanding officer, killed in action. I can't tell you much about the first regiment because I wasn't there but the second regiment spent the first three months of the war in Fife. We were stationed two squadrons in Markinch and two in Leslie, and in the first months of the war, we used to patrol the ground from Elie to Anstruther and Crail at night in case the Germans landed. They bombed Rosyth in October 1939. I remember seeing the bombers over the Forth Road Bridge. I was up behind Dunfermline at the time. We had our officers mess in the house of Anderson's, the paper mill people at the west end of Leslie. We were there for the first three and a half months of the war from September to mid January of 1940 when we went to Aldershot to the barracks which the first regiment had left when they went to France. We were stationed there and getting ready to go to Europe as reinforcements. When the fall of France came, we moved out of Aldershot into Farnham because the Canadians had arrived and they wanted proper barracks, so we were put out to live in digs while the Canadians took over our barracks in Aldershot. When France fell we were ready to go abroad and I was on duty at two o'clock in the morning when a chap arrived on a motor bicycle with a message which said 'Prepare to move to unknown destination at twenty four hours notice.' Underneath it said 'Copy to Northern Ireland District Belfast', but in fact we went to Dungannon which is right in the centre of Northern Ireland. We then had a squadron stationed in the grounds of Field Marshal Alexander's home which was right on the border with South of Ireland and we stayed there through the summer of 1940 in case the Germans, having occupied the whole of France, decided to invade through Ireland.

We stayed there until May or June 1941, having been the divisional cavalry regiment .We then became part of the 11th armoured division which was a new division formed with the two new regiments, the 23rd Hussars and the 24th Lancers which didn't exist pre-war and we became the 29th Armoured Brigade of the 11th Armoured Division.

We were stationed in Yorkshire at Whitby and the Germans dropped bombs on Yorkshire moors quite often when they were trying to bomb Middlesbrough. We used to have to go and put out fires in the middle of the night. There were steel works in Middlesbrough which they were aiming for. I was Acting Captain at the beginning of the war and became an Acting Major but still got a Captain's pay. That happened to a lot of people. We moved to Brighton and were on the south coast, on the downs, then Bury St Edmonds and various other places preparing to go abroad.

The King and Queen visited the regiment in Aldershot. This was leading up to D Day, June 1944 when the invasion took place. We landed in Normandy about two weeks after the invasion and fought our way through Normandy, and then we led the advance that finished up in Antwerp at the time that the Guards Armoured Division arrived in Brussels.

King George VI inspecting the regiment at Aldershot

At the time of the Arnhem Bridge battle, when they dropped an enormous number of parachutists, we were in reserve and didn't take any part in that. We saw it from a distance as you might say. Soon after that we went up into various parts of Holland and I became second in command of the regiment, gave up B Squadron which I'd been commanding till then and became second in command to Alec Scott. We spent the autumn in Holland. Shortly before Christmas we handed in our tanks and headed down to Ypres in Belgium where we were to be refitted with a new British tank, the Comet. I remember being woken at two in the morning by someone who had just arrived to tell us we must go back and collect our old tanks because the Germans had attacked through Ardennes. We landed up in Bruges to hold the bridges over the river Meuse. We were then involved in counter attacks in the Ardennes with the armoured airborne divisions that had come in.

When that was over we went back to Ypres to refit with the new tanks ready for the crossing of the Rhine. We were about two days after the original attack crossing the Rhine and went up through Germany. I was wounded outside the horrible camp at Belsen and was in hospital for about six weeks or so and landed home on leave the day the war ended. I was invalided out. When the regiment was reformed after the war, I became the first commanding officer. One regiment was disbanded after the war; the other was based here in Fife, later amalgamated with the Scottish Horse and is now part of the Queen's Own Yeomanry. A lot of the squadron have served in Ireland, Bosnia and Iraq.

The old Montrave House was a hospital during the war mainly for Polish servicemen. It was run by my step-mother who kept them under control. We got a lot of people I can remember when I was home on leave – people in the Merchant Navy operating out of Methil with convoys down to London, and wounded or sick men from the convoys in the Firth of Forth. Old Montrave House, which was demolished around 1970, was ideally sized and situated for a hospital. It was a vast warren of a place, with over a hundred rooms, too big to live in but great big rooms ideal for hospital wards. The house had been rebuilt in 1870; before that, it had been a smallish house with a chapel attached. The air raid shelter for the hospital is still there.

Polish Troops, the 5th Polish Airborne Division, were billeted at Largo House and they built a tower at Lundin Tower to practice parachute jumping. It was said that more Poles were killed or injured jumping off the tower than by the Germans.

A German bomber dropped two or three bombs on the top field here at Montrave and on Durie. The stay behind the bunker built at Durie which is still there would have been used by commandos in case of invasion. There was an anti-tank ditch dug across the middle of Fife, with a number of pill boxes which ran through Ladybank woods and went down through Markinch. All beaches were considered ideal landing places if the Germans invaded through Norway and the Lundin Links pill box is still there. There were great concrete boxes all along the beach and though most have been destroyed. There were very big gun emplacements just below the golf club at Lundin Links, Anstruther and Elie, and big coastal defences because the Forth was boomed off.'

After the war, Sir John continued his distinguished career. He became Battalion Commander in 1950, was appointed Captain of The Royal Company of Archers and Honorary Colonel of The Highland Yeomanry RAC, T& AVR. He served as Conservative Member of Parliament for East Fife 1961 – 1979 and was Chairman of the Conservative and Unionist Party in Scotland 1965 – 1967; Lord Lieutenant of Fife from 1980 –1987 and Lord High Commissioner of The General Assembly 1982 – 1983.

Sir John's son, also John Gilmour, joined the regiment in 1965 and is now the Honorary Colonel, following the family tradition. Though too young to remember the war, he too had stories to tell.

'During the war a gentleman called George Cocker was my grandfather's agent. The estate office was at Balcormo and there was a tin shed where George worked. When George retired, Dad went down to clear it out and bring everything up to Montrave. They found four incendiary bombs which a German bomber had dropped in the field below the farm.

George had found them and instead of getting rid of them he put them in the cupboard under the safe in the office and they had sat there from 1941 or 1942 until 1950.

The bomb disposal squad came along and took them away to blow up. Quite a long time later, I think 1972, I was clearing a burn and the digger driver unearthed a bomb along with a scoop full of mud. It fell on its fins underneath the digger but luckily it didn't go off. I have the fins as a paperweight in my office.'

Air Raid Wardens, possibly at Kirkland Drive, Leven

JIM HAMILTON

Jim Hamilton is a world famous pigeon fancier having won innumerable championships and awards. The eldest of seven children, Jim was born in the Maw, a small group of cottages along the Standing Stane Road, on 1st March 1920, and moved to Aberhill when he was eight. He was nineteen and working for Simpsons the grocers in Leven in 1939.

'The day war broke out I was at Cameron Bridge cleaning out my pigeons when my grandfather came and told me. I joined the army in December and went to the Black Watch Queen's Barracks in Perth in January. From there I went to Orkney for a year with the RASC, serving units in the Orkneys, near where the *Royal Oak* was sunk. A spell at Hawick where we were billeted in an old mill lasted about two years then, in April 1943, by which time I'd been promoted to sergeant, we were sent to Nigeria.

Our task was to form what would become the 82nd West Africa Division, from a nucleus of Nigerians and Gold Coasters. I soon realised that many could speak no English, and I didn't speak their language, so I had at least to pick up a small vocabulary. It made a terrific difference and I got on very well with them. It made the troops happier that somebody could understand them. There were a number of dialects but Hausa was the common language.

The 82nd Division headed for the docks at Lagos where we embarked for Gibraltar. At that time, the Germans had not been quite cleared out of the Mediterranean so we hugged the shore all the way, so close you could throw a stone on to the beach. We got through the Suez Canal into the Red Sea and one of our ships full of soldiers went aground. Our ship was used to ferry them to Aden, then we proceeded to Karachi, where we boarded a steam train full of African troops with just a few Europeans.

The journey from Karachi to Calcutta took seven days and was amusing but not comfortable. The Europeans were able to phone ahead to the next stop so we could have a bath and a feed. It wasn't so easy for the Africans, so we had to devise a way of keeping them clean. The engines required water at every stop so we marched the men in a long column, bar of soap in hand, under the water tower and they were handed towels at the other end. The Indian ladies kept their distance but were very interested in the proceedings.

After six weeks camping in a mining area in Behar, we went by boat to Chittagong. We created a big camp in North Burma and were given the job of clearing the Japanese from the seaward side of the Arakan. Fortunately the Japs had been turned, by the 14th Army. We had three brigades, about twenty thousand men, and lost a lot of them . By this time the war in Europe was over and the Burma Campaign was of no interest to people after VE Day. We were called the Forgotten Army and had it bad, but it could have been worse. The Africans loved their uniforms but boots were a problem. In training in Nigeria, we had to get them into boots. They weren't comfortable but we told them they'd have to persevere because of the diseases they could pick up in the jungle. The first time we had any real trouble in Burma, we were travelling on very narrow tracks, and one day we came across an area that was covered with boots. We were operating in an area where the Japanese were, and whenever the men were under pressure, and the nearer we got to the enemy, the more they took their boots off.

We lost a lot of magnificent men because they preferred the machete to the rifle. I was fortunate. I went in and came out – others didn't last a fortnight. What kept me alive in the combat area for over a year was dark rum. I washed with it, cleaned my teeth with it, diluted of course, and drank it. My water bottle always contained a percentage of rum. I had worked alongside marine commandos and picked up the tip from them.

The supporting of our division with supplies was difficult in the jungle terrain especially when we had, from time to time, to rely on supply drops by Dakota planes. The versatility of the suppliers knew no bounds and anything from pairs of socks to a welcome feed of roast chicken came tumbling from the sky.

We finished up at a camp about twenty miles from Rangoon and my job as Staff Sergeant Major was to arrange transport for men going home. I saw some hellish sights. I was going in there from the north and the prisoners were coming from the Burma Railway and other camps in the East. There were some poor souls. Then it was my turn to get on a boat. I had done some studying in my spare time and when I got home I joined Fife County Council Assessor's Department.'

What Jim didn't say was that he had been mentioned in dispatches for distinguished service, but he was proud of his role as a member of the National Pigeon Service. Like many other pigeon fanciers Jim provided pigeons for wartime service with the air force and other military organizations . During the war, over two hundred and fifty thousand racing pigeons were used and thirty two of them were awarded the Dickin Medal, the animal equivalent of the Victoria Cross. The pigeons were used by the Royal Corps of Signals and, as well as the National Pigeon Service, there was a Pigeon Policy Committee there and an Air Ministry Pigeon Section.

'I went off to war in 1940, and the first time I came home on leave, there were young birds in the loft. They were being bred for Leuchars, where there was an establishment for young birds. When they were trained, they went on planes Every war plane that left Leuchars or any other airport in the country carried two pigeons. If the plane came down and they were liberated, experts could tell how far they had flown and so could help pinpoint where survivors might be located. The birds carried a message which was transmitted to Leuchars who would know which plane they had come from. One pigeon, Winkie got home to Broughty Ferry from a plane that was known to have come down, and the expert was able to say they were looking in the wrong place. The area of search was changed and eight survivors were found.

Through the National Pigeon Service, pigeon breeders trained and supplied birds to the army, air force, home guard, police and other services. Pigeons also went to Normandy with the invasion forces. A trip across the channel is nothing to these birds. They were dropped behind enemy lines and worked with secret agents, bringing back information and micro-photographs. They were often wounded and many were killed in action.'

Home Guard exercise with an armoured train

EDWARD JONES

Eddie Jones spent thirty four years in the mining industry. Born in 1920, he left school at fourteen and began work at the pit head. Three months later he was working underground. When the war started he tried to join the navy but was rejected.

'Both my brother and my father were in the navy, and I went to Edinburgh to join up, but when I said I was a miner, they sent me home again. The miners who got accepted had either left the mines or said they had. If I'd said I was a joiner or a plumber, I'd have got away. My father was a miner but he had left the pit the year before and was building the aerodrome at Leuchars. My other brother left the mines and joined the army but I was left to do away in the pit.

It was the Wemyss Coal Company at the time and working conditions were terrible, you couldn't describe them.

I worked on my back or on my side in seams less than four feet. I've been trapped underground quite often and had to work our way out. They didn't have the same supports for the roof then. It was wooden pit props and it was a long time before they got the steel ones. The situation was terrible but the comradeship was perfect, it was really good. We didn't have pit baths, you had to go home in your working clothes and there was no hot water or central heating, just one fire where your pit clothes had to be dried. There was a lot of pressure on us to produce coal for the war effort, and we were down the pit when the bombs dropped here.

I was in the Rosie Pit to begin with, then the Michael. I stayed there till it went on fire. Luckily I had a wedding on the day of the disaster so had a day off.

My father was in the navy all though the war. He helped attend the injured on board ship and he got a medal, I think it was the BEM. My youngest brother was killed. He was a steward on a boat that got bombed.'

Levenmouth at War

DESRENEE IRVINE

Ron Irvine, née Desrenée North, was living in Yorkshire when the war started. She thought she would like to join the A.T.S. (Auxiliary Territorial Service) because she had been born in the Army, but her father suggested that she try the W.A.A.F. (Women's Auxiliary Air Force) instead, because they had better looking stockings.

Just after the Battle of Britain, when I was sixteen, we had been for a holiday in Blackpool; all the boarding house owners had to billet their share of RAF recruits. When I was seventeen and a half I wanted to get away from home, to see the world. Working in my father's sub-post office seemed very dull. My mother didn't want me to go, but my dad signed the papers so she couldn't do anything about it. I joined up in November 1941, and the train from Leeds picked up new recruits at many stations on the way down to Gloucester. We spent four days at RAF Innsworth, where the Ministry of Defence now keeps the records of all ex-service personnel.

Here we were taught basic marching drill although we were still in civilian clothes and some of us were inappropriately dressed, and wearing high heeled shoes. We were given medical checks and aptitude tests, and decisions were made about which trade we would go into. Because I'd worked in the post office, they put me into Pay Accounts. It was not exactly what I would have liked to do, but better than the cookhouse, transport or being a general dogsbody. After being kitted out we were sent to Morecombe, another seaside resort crowded with RAF rookies, for a four-week square-bashing course, marching up and down on the prom. I had more medicals, inoculations for tetanus etc., was vaccinated against smallpox then sent to Penarth near Cardiff for a six-week course in The Ship Inn which had been commandeered, this time on pay accounts and ledgers. We were billeted in a posh, Victorian grey stone house. The daughter of the house was willing to take two young girls who didn't smoke. At the end of the course we were graded as Leading Aircraft Woman (LACW) or ordinary Aircraft Woman (ACW1 or ACW2) and could be posted anywhere in the U.K.

I was sent to Bridlington, to the Spa Hotel, which had been taken over as the Accounts Section for the RAF unit there. It was forty over-staffed, so people hung around for weeks, doing nothing very much, until they were posted somewhere else. In April 1942 I was posted to 60 OTU at East Fortune near North Berwick. In this Operational Training Unit, young cadets, the future aircrew for fighters and bombers, were trained to fly. Sometimes, if they were flying into a haar, they forgot about the North Berwick Law and crashed into it.

Like most airfields, East Fortune covered a huge area. We were billeted in the wards of a former tuberculosis sanatorium known as the Sanatorium Site, and were issued with bicycles to get from site to site. The cookhouse and mess hall were on the other site, known as Flights, on the far side of the airfield, now the Museum of Flight, where they serviced aeroplanes and trainee aircrew waited in dispersal huts to take off. We had to cycle around or across the airfield and back three times a day for meals, and sometimes, especially if it was windy, we would go outside the camp and round by the road through Athelstaneford. The verges and hedgerows were full of wild flowers, and rabbits would scamper across our path. In Autumn, when the corn was being harvested, we wore ground sheets when cycling around by the road to protect us from the clouds of black harvest insects which descended upon us.

There was a severe frost on 1st May, 1942, and on that day the heating was turned off, and we sat in our overcoats and gloves, cuddling hot water bottles and doing accounts. A fortnight later, I spent four days in sickbay because I had fallen asleep in the sun and got badly sunburned. The sick bay was in Gilmerton House, a beautiful old country house with a square staircase with wonderful old oil portraits on the walls. This was my first glimpse of how the other half lived. If you got sick, and it was considered to be your own fault, you could be put on a charge and punished. It was your own fault if you got sunburnt. The M.O. (Medical Officer) let me off and did not put me on a charge.

I met my future husband at East Fortune, though I was much too young to think about such matters then. Jim was born in Kilsyth. His father was a miner, whose eyes had been damaged by ironstone mining; he received no compensation. Jim's mother was a schoolteacher and was offered a job at St. Agatha's, so the family came to Methil to live. Before the war Jim was recruited by examination into the Civil Service after he left Buckhaven High School, and was sent to Woolwich Arsenal. This was a great shock after a quiet home life in Methil. Here he accounted for guns, bullets, munitions and all things military needed by a nation shortly to be at war. He was conscripted into the RAF in 1941.

Whilst at East Fortune, we went to the pictures occasionally, or out for a meal, usually beans on toast, in a cafe in North Berwick called *The Ancient Grudge*. You couldn't get much in restaurants then, food was scarce, but if you were lucky you could get eggs, chips and peas for half a crown, that is, two shillings and sixpence or 12½ p, at *The Parachute Cafe* which was outside the main gate at the Drem airfield, three miles from East Fortune.

RAF policy was to re-train personnel, where possible, for trades of greater importance to the war effort. Jim was not happy about being a stores accounts clerk, and so he applied for a course as a wireless mechanic. While waiting to be posted – part of the course was done at RAF Cardington the other part at Glasgow Technical College, now a University, he was allowed over to Flights to see how the wireless mechanics worked. Occasionally he would tell the Stores Accounts that he was at Flights and tell Flights that he was at Stores, when actually he was in a corner of the airfield somewhere reading a book and smoking his pipe. This wasn't discovered until his posting arrived and he couldn't be found at either place.

By this time, I had been posted to RAF Wittering, near Peterborough, a fighter station in 12 Group, and was there for about a year. It was the best station I was ever on, until they decided we needed smartening up, and put us on regular drill training at 6 p.m. after a hard day's work.

Sometimes we marched up and down on the beginning of the runway. Occasionally bombers that could not get back to their own bases put down at Wittering, which had very long runways, and the crews who had to stay for a few days, would come into the Accounts Section for a sub on their pay-books. One evening when we were marching on the beginning of the runway a Lancaster bomber came taxi-ing towards us. The W.A.A.F. officer in charge didn't seem too sure what to do but eventually got her wits together and ordered us to 'About Turn' and we marched back the way we had come.

At Wittering I dealt with WAAF accounts and with those of one of the flights –BAT Flight, Beam Approach Training Flight. I think it was something to do with guiding in the aircraft to the flare paths in foggy weather. Men were sent from all over the country to do this course.

The girls were billeted in what had been the married quarters in peacetime, semi-detached houses with the perimeter fence between us and the Great North Road. We didn't have far to walk to the Accounts Section so at Wittering we were not issued with bikes.

Pay parades were held once a fortnight. Pay was calculated to the nearest florin (two shilling piece) to which the individual was entitled. An advance was made when a person was going on leave. Pay was calculated according to rank and trade, with any additional amount such as long service payment, or danger money, something enjoyed by the

Service Police under the rank of Corporal. Money was deducted for voluntary payments to wives and mothers etc, for National Insurance, for Income Tax, or as punishment for misdemeanours, once a quarter for barrack damages. Everyone had to share in the repair bill for barrack damages, and this deduction was always resented.

It was the pay accounts clerk's job to work out the pay and to decide precisely the number of each denomination of coin you would require, to be able to give everyone the exact amount they were due on the Pay Parade. This process was known as Coining. It had a special form for the purpose. Pay Parades were held in suitable buildings, quite often a hangar. The Accountant Officer had the cash on the table before him, the Pay clerk to his right with the Pay form, with Witnessing Officers to either side. The assembled recipients, standing at ease, would be brought to attention. The Pay clerk would call out the name of the first person, who would reply "Sir", followed the last three digits of his service number, advance towards the table, come to attention, salute the Accountant Officer, the Pay Clerk would call out the amount to be paid, the Accountant would place the amount to the front of the table, the airman would sign for it, do a smart about turn, and return to his former place. The whole process would be repeated until all had received their pay. The pay form was completed with the signatures of the three officers. The amounts paid would later be inked in, in the Pay Ledger.

The pay ledgers were balanced up once a quarter; we then opened up new ledgers and transferred the details across. This procedure meant that we had to work until ten o'clock every night for about a month. We were always short of staff so eventually the powers that be changed the ledger transfers to once every four months.

Life in the Armed Forces was governed by King's Regulations. Under KR's. the Adjutant would issue a D.R.O. (Daily Routine Order) which covered everything that any section of the station would need to know in order to function, such as parades to be held, or who had been promoted, married, chucked out, (KR 652 clause 11—pregnancy – married and single), gone AWOL (absent without leave), gone sick, who was posted in or posted out from one RAF station to another, on leave, etc. Each Section took from this Order details that affected it. This Order had to be read everyday by everybody. Ignorance was no excuse.

In Accounts, we entered the information in the relevant Pay Ledger in the Remarks column against the serving man or woman, and took action in the appropriate column. If you had been deemed guilty of a charge against you, you could have your pay deducted. Some language used by deserters to the Special Police, e.g. "B....r off, you stupid b.....d", could not of course be repeated in Orders and, under KR's, the following archaic phrase had to be substituted and the report would read something like this: 'On being apprehended by the Special Police, Cpl. Bloggs replied, "You may do as you like", he said, "but I will soldier no more".' After which he would be taken into custody and charged with desertion. I thought this was hilarious.

One day a ludicrous order was published; in future men and women were not to talk to each other outside work on camp; we were at a loss to understand this. All became clear with the sudden arrival of the American Army Air Force. Some high-up Blimp had issued this order to prevent fraternisation. It couldn't be enforced, though they tried. We had camp dances once a fortnight and men would escort their dancing partners back to the WAAF quarters, via the path alongside a field hedged by some bushes. The WAAF Admin staff accompanied by some Special Police would follow and root out snogging couples, take their names and put them on a charge.

The Americans were, on the whole, homesick and didn't want to be here. They spoke English, of a sort, but with different intonation, accent and idiom, but we got by. We got tired of this stupid nonsense about not speaking to men on camp, tired of the simulated gas attacks and having to work in the gas masks, just to get used to them. They were horribly steamy things. We also got tired of the marching.

I volunteered for a posting, to Coltishall, another fighter station in 12 Group, this time in East Anglia, a few minutes flying time from Nazi occupied Holland, a few minutes flying time for a German night Fighter to follow one of ours in and shoot up the airfield.

When D Day came, on 6th June 1944, men were sent to Europe, and special Base Account Units were set up to deal with this. I was posted to one of these at RAF Clifton, York, where we were billeted in Nissen huts which were made of corrugated iron and were not insulated. It was bitterly cold on the plain of York in the winter of 1944/45. Outside chemical toilets meant we had to stagger out on cold, windy nights; baths were in a remote farm building – two baths with cold-water taps, and we carried the hot water from an open topped boiler with a bucket.

It was so cold that in the morning the bicycles did not work and we had to take them into the hut to thaw them out, so that the chain connected with the chain wheel. The hut itself was only warm because thirty people slept in it. There was little fuel for the stoves. One girl had a large bottle of ink on the shelf, and it shattered leaving a bottle-shaped lump of ice.

The war in Europe ended while I was in York and shortly after that the unit was transferred to Innsworth and I applied for an overseas posting, now that I was twenty one. I went first to the Wirral, and, after embarkation leave, to Southampton to board a wonderful P.and O. liner, which had been converted into a troop ship, the *Strathaird*. Officers were in first class, we women (other ranks) in second, and men (other ranks), sleeping in hammocks, in steerage below decks.

We landed in Algiers in July 1945 and were billeted in a commercial college with trees in the garden. The trees were full of ants. Our food was full of them also, ants in the peas and in the bread, which was made by Italian prisoners of war. The flour was adulterated with chalk and the bread was dark brown with chalky lumps in it. Much of the meat was horsemeat. Conditions were bad; horses, cows and sheep were so thin that some dropped dead on their way to market. The Arabs used to flog them in an attempt to make them get up, giving a more vivid meaning to the expression 'flogging a dead horse'.

I was in the WAAF for five years, and once abroad I did not get home until August 1946. It had taken a long time to assemble the armed forces and scatter them over the globe and it took a long time to pull them back and send them home. It would not have been wise to demobilise everyone at the same time, even if it could have been done, as it would have been very difficult for them to be integrated into civilian life; better little by little. After a life in the services it took a long time to get used to life in civvy street. Most of all I missed the comradeship that had existed.'

Britain was not the only place where women had to queue.
Here Arab women line up in Algiers

BUCKHAVEN'S SECRET TRAGEDY

The following report from The East Fife Mail of June 5th, 1991, marked the 50th anniversary of one of the worst tragedies ever to strike the Levenmouth area.

'This disaster which resulted in the death of ten people, eight of them children, was never made public and, outside the community affected, few could share the grief or offer comfort to the families.

Despite the tension of the war years when every home offered up prayers for a loved one serving their country, Monday, June 2nd, 1941, provided an opportunity to relax with neighbours as the area celebrated the Fife Miners Gala. But this particular year, the horror of war and its destruction was to be cruelly delivered on to an unsuspecting community's doorstep.

In Buckhaven, Gala Day brought the children out in force, especially for the parade, the highlight of the day's events.

Some of the youngsters were already out and about, down on a part of the shore known locally as the 'Jawbanes', playing, skiffing stones, keeping an eye open for some sea coal to fuel the evening fire.

What exactly happened next remains unclear. What is known is that a group of lads found something lying by the water's edge - distant witnesses reckoned it was cylinder-shaped- and the youngsters began to haul it clear.

Some said they were dragging it across the nearby cobbled stable yard; others that it was lifted upright or was being loaded into a cart. No one is completely sure, but everyone remembers the explosion which I shook the buildings and shattered the heart of a community.

Bill Phenix was editor of the Leven Mail at the time of the incident and accustomed to the stringent reporting restrictions imposed during the war years but even he was astonished at the tight security blanket thrown around the tragedy. Whether it was to avoid a blow to a war-ravaged nation's morale or in the interests of defence, outside the stunned community, life went on as normal.

Most of those who died in the horrific explosion were laid to rest in the parish cemetery at East Wemyss where simple headstones give no clue to the tragic circumstances of their death. The only acknowledgement permitted appeared in a provincial daily newspaper at the end of the week which stated the provost of the burgh had launched a disaster fund. Any subsequent inquiry into that 'disaster' went unreported in the local community. The families which suffered a loss were left to be comforted by their neighbours and the tragedy became Buckhaven's secret.

With no official records readily accessible, Buckhaven has kept the names of the victims to itself for fifty years. Those who have researched the incident, notably Bill Phenix, have provided the Mail, half a century on, with the following list of those believed to have been the casualties:

Robert Birrell (31) George Irvine (13); George (15) and Robert Jensen (14) Joe (13) and William Kinnear (10), John Thomson (12), Henry Walton (14), Henry (37) and James Wilkie (13).'

In fact, the Leven Mail of June 11th 1941, gave the names of the killed and injured . The report reads :

'Eight men and two boys were killed when an explosion occurred at an East Scotland town on Monday of last week. There is only one survivor of the incident, a fifty four year old man who was slightly injured. The dead include two pairs of brothers and a father and son. Two horses were also killed, one inside a stable, the other which was yoked to the cart. The only survivor had a remarkable escape from serious injury. He was inside the stable when the explosion took place and was partially protected by some wooden partitions. He was allowed home after medical treatment. First Aid personnel were soon on the scene and rendered assistance. Further attention was given to some casualties at the First Aid Post, and First Aid ambulances soon took those still alive to hospital.'

The survivor was James Lomax. The names of those killed are inscribed on Methil War Memorial. One person who had vivid memories of that day was Myra Frantz who was seven years old at the time:

'It was the second day of June and the Gala Day. There was hustle and bustle in my house that morning. we were all getting ready to go to the Gala. We were hurrying so we could join in the parade. I had finished whitening my sandshoes and they were sparkling white again. My dress was a new one bought specially for that day. I had a nice new satin ribbon for my hair too. I felt really pretty that day. Auntie Ruby and cousin Maureen. who lived with us then. were also going to the Gala. Maureen was only three and she too was all dressed up in a new cotton frock. But what she wanted most of all was to see the band and asked over and over again for this.

I just wished everyone would hurry up so we could all get going. It would soon be time for the parade to start. I didn't want to miss anything. I had arranged to meet my chums, too. We were going to run in the races. We would all get our bag of buns, mince pies and a bottle of milk. Oh, it was going to be a great day. I thought.

At that moment there was the most terrifying loud bang. The house seemed to shudder and groan. The windows cracked and a few actually shattered to pieces. I yelled for my mum and Maureen started to cry. My mother and aunt came running into the living room and grabbed us. We were both crying now and very frightened.

'Have the Germans landed?' I asked. 'What made that terrible bang. will I have to wear my gas mask?'

My mother left me with my aunt and wee cousin and went off to investigate. There was an urgent knock at the door. My aunt answered it to our downstairs neighbour. Mrs Webster.

'I think you should all come down to my house till we see what is happening,' she said. 'If it is an air raid or something, you will be better on the ground floor.'

So we went downstairs to wait, and wait we did... it seemed like forever. Meantime, while we waited, we amused ourselves with the new baby grand–daughter, Dorothea. When finally my mother and my aunt came back they seemed quite upset, pale-faced and trembling. There had been an explosion down on the beach and they wanted to go down to see if Agnes, Bobby and the boys, who had gone out earlier, were alright.

Mrs. Webster knew what was on their minds and right away offered to look after us. We stayed there for quite some time, playing with the baby. Maureen decided she preferred the teddy bear instead. I was allowed to hold the baby and feed her. It was all new to me, but I remember liking it. Finally, after what seemed like hours, my mother and aunt returned more upset than they had been before. This time, they were in tears. They sat talking to Mrs Webster, trying to tell what had happened. I could tell from what they were saying that something terrible had occurred down near the stables at the beach.

Some boys had dragged what they thought was a piece of scrap metal across the beach. They had been collecting scrap for the war effort. My Uncle Bobby had a stable, horses and a sea coal business. He was having his usual blether with the scaffy when he saw the boys. He shouted to them to 'get rid of that thing,' as it didn't look safe. But dragging it over the cobbled stable yard proved fatal. It exploded, causing havoc and mayhem. The old houses withstood the blast from the mine but their walls were embedded with pieces of metal and shrapnel. There had been ten boys and men at the stables that morning. Eight died immediately. The huge wooden doors were blown off and, inside, two horses died where they stood, There was a huge crater in the yard, boulders everywhere, The hay and oats were scattered like a carpet over the stable floor, the oat boxes were lying in smithereens, harnesses and carts were totally destroyed. It was a scene of complete disaster. The skaffy, who was inside the stable at the time of the blast filling up his water can to make tea, was the only one to survive. He had missed the full force of the explosion.

My uncle was taken across the road to his house to await the ambulance He was terribly injured but how badly was not apparent until later. All doctors who were available were there. Then the ambulances came. The police had a terrible time trying to control the crowds of people. Mothers and fathers were all running around trying to find their boys. There was panic in the streets that day.

The beach and stables were popular places and there were always boys playing about. Many of them picked sea coal for their own homes. My Cousins, Jim and Archie, weren't at the stable that morning with their dad otherwise they might have been among the victims. Jim had been waiting for his pal to see about the gala, and Archie who was very young, was sleeping late.

The police allowed my mother and my aunt past the barricade into my Aunt Agnes' house. She, by this time, was in a terrible state. Uncle Bobby was bleeding badly and they were trying to get him on to a stretcher. He kept saying he was all right but it was obvious to the three sisters that he wasn't. The other young man died the next day.

Uncle Bobby asked for his shaving things to be brought in to him in hospital. He said he was feeling lucky he had survived it all. But his things were never needed again. He died on June 4, 1941. The horrific episode had claimed its eighth victim.

On the day of the mass funeral, a company of Polish soldiers stationed in Leven were out on a march which happened to coincide with the departure of the hearses. They stood to attention and gave a salute. The streets of Buckhaven were lined with people that day and the crowds seemed to stretch all the way to East Wemyss and to the cemetery. Many were school chums of the boys who died. It was a sight never to be forgotten. June is here again and half a century has passed. I often think of the unforgettable day all that time ago, of the people who died and the people who survived to grieve for their loved ones, of a community that was blown to pieces and has never been the same again.'

Levenmouth at War

THE WEST WEMYSS TRAGEDY

The report of the Buckhaven disaster in the East Fife Mail prompted Atta Graham, who has lived in East Wemyss for forty years, to remind people of another incident which claimed the lives of five people on January 23, 1941, five months before the Buckhaven tragedy. On February 5th that year, the Leven Mail reported a Ministry of Home Security report that 'Inhabitants of a Scottish town saw a mine floating near the shore. They pulled it in, it exploded, killing three men and injuring two.'

The mine exploded near Lady's Rock in West Wemyss, killing fifteen year old Peter Graham and four miners.

The Mail spoke to Andrew Walker, who as a young surveyor at the Wemyss estate office Red House was literally yards away from the site of the accident. He recalled that in those days, miners would walk along the foreshore to the Michael Pit.

'I think a chap happened to look out and see something bobbing about in the sea. A group of men decided to lasso the thing and bring it into shore because they might have been worried about it hitting a boat in the Forth.'

The men had caught the mine with ropes and were dragging it in when Peter joined them. The mine was brought ashore but, it was suggested, one of its spikes caught on a rock and it exploded. Peter and three of the men died instantly, one survived for two days. Andrew Walker said that secrecy was common, and the incident was hushed up. The authorities did not want people to know mines were coming ashore. Like the Buckhaven victims, the West Wemyss gravestones give no indication of the cause of death. Peter's just gives his name and the other reads 'George Storrar, who died as a result of an accident 23rd January, 1941.'

Atta Graham was able to fill in some of the details of the story of this wartime tragedy. Born and brought up in Glasgow, Atta used to spend holidays with her aunt in West Wemyss, where she got to know the Graham family.

'I was Peter's girl friend when I was fifteen. We used to write each other and went to the pictures together.

I was told that men got money for taking in mines; some people said they just took them in for safety but I can't see that they'd risk their lives for nothing. Peter's brother Robbie and his mother were sitting in the kitchen when the bomb went off. Peter had gone out the door only five minutes before. Mother asked him where he was going and he said, 'You'd awful like to know, wouldn't you?' He was actually going to MacGregor's shop for sweeties, the new ration was just in.

When the bomb went off they were flung across the floor. Father ran out and saw Peter's bike against the dyke and Peter was dead, his arms and legs off. He shouted to Robbie to keep Mother away, take her back to the house.

Peter had just started the Home Guard, he'd gone with Robbie to Edinburgh to join up but he was just sixteen and they told him to come back in a year. Robbie joined up that day and was five years in the air force. Peter decided to join the Home Guard till he was old enough to join up. He was a big handsome boy of sixteen, six foot tall, it was such a waste. He came from a good and loving family and his mother was never the same after that. His family worked at the castle and Her Ladyship insisted that Peter be coffined and lie in the chapel there, but his mother pleaded for him to be taken home. She didn't want him to be lying up there alone so the coffin was carried down through the trees. Peter's twelve year old Alsatian Gyp wouldn't come out from under his coffin and had to be put down. It was a very sad time.

My mother got a phone call to tell us what had happened. We lived right by the River Clyde and we didn't have shelters because of the kind of tenement we lived in so we used to run across the road to my uncle's carrying our gas masks and the dog. It was bad running across the road with the bombs dropping and the ack ack guns firing. You could hear the planes, the Germans had a different sound to ours and one night a bomb went down the funnel of a ship. We were evacuated but luckily it was a dud or it would have blown up the Clyde. I remember the nights Clydebank got blitzed, you could see the flames shooting up. Churchill stood at the top of Kilbowie Hill in Clydebank and wept at the devastation.

You just accepted it, you got up and went to your work past the buildings that had been destroyed. I remember a stretcher coming out of a house and there was a mother and a baby on it and they were both dead. The most frightening thing was the guns out in the street, making the buildings shake. One night, we were up five times, you'd just get back into bed and the siren would go again. The dog would wake us up because he heard it before we did.

The Graham family always treated me like royalty because I'd been Peter's girl friend, and once when I was on holiday, Robbie was home on leave and we started going out together. We got married in 1947 and rationing was still going on. My mother saved up tins of stew and got the baker to provide pastry for pies. It was the worst winter for forty years, our taxi got stuck in the snow and my silk stockings, a special present from my sister, were in tatters. We had a spree in the village here and everyone gave little thing like clothes pegs and so on.

I remember VE Day, seeing the rockets from the *Sneland* and *Avondale* going up. Everyone thought it was part of the celebrations. It was a very close community, one for all and all for one.

Peter and the other victims have never been mentioned all these years and I don't think it has been recorded. There was never a thing done about it. They should be honoured before their story is completely forgotten. It was tragic for a wee village like Wemyss.'

THE FLYING ANGEL

The Mission for Seamen, which cares for the spiritual and practical welfare of seafarers of all races and creeds and their families, arrived in Methil on November 22nd, 1939. Like the rest of their centres, it was known as The Flying Angel, from the flag which flies over all the mission centres and is instantly recognised by seamen of all nationalities. It was inspired by the verse from the Book of Revelations, Chapter 14 verse 6: *'Then I saw an angel flying in mid-heaven, with an eternal gospel to proclaim to those on earth, to every nation and tribe, language and people.'*

The history of the Mission, which has branches throughout the world, and is not connected with any specific church, dates back to 1835 when John Ashley, a young Anglican clergyman began a ministry among seamen. His work continues and the flag carrying the logo of the flying angel and the words 'Missions to Seamen' still flies over all mission centres and is instantly recognised by seamen of all nationalities. Originally launches were needed to take chaplains to visit ships at anchor and to bring seamen ashore, but eventually ships could come alongside as soon as they arrived in port. The Flying Angel clubs were then built to provide not only reading rooms and a chapel but sleeping accommodation and light refreshments as well as spiritual sustenance. Seamen not only from the merchant ships but naval personnel were glad to find the facilities offered by the clubs. The proud boast of the organisation was that the sun never set on the Flying Angel. According to a spokesman, 'Members go aboard ships to visit seamen, go out into the roads and come into port with them. On shore we provide him with a home from home, answer the seaman's need for friendship. If he is in hospital unable to understand the language, we visit him and explain everything.'

During the two world wars the mission centres were of course very busy and Methil was no exception, with coal, its chief export, assuming terrific importance. The mission came to Methil because of conditions created by the war – fifteen hundred to two thousand sailors in port and the only facilities were the pubs in the High Street. In an article in 1942 The Chaplain gave an account of its work:

'It was on the 22nd November, 1939, that we arrived at this port on the east coast of Fife, and a few days later took a house on the main street and hoisted our flag and people began to ask who was this stranger who called himself the *Flying Angel*. We hired a lorry and made expeditions into the countryside, calling on some of the influential residents, and soon had a load of furniture of sorts with which to open house. My wife and I lived in one room, all the others being devoted to the seamen, and the maid's room we turned into a little chapel, although it would only hold about a dozen men. The sailors hailed us with delight, and what a strange house we kept! Sometimes the men overflowed into all rooms, even to sitting round the gas cooker, offering advice when meals were being prepared.

These were very happy days, both for us and for the men, and our neighbours were often disturbed from their slumbers at midnight by the singing of our evening hymn in the tiny church, before the men would leave us to snatch a few hours sleep... these were very happy days and we were genuinely sorry when the time came that the ever increasing numbers of men forced us to seek larger and more convenient premises...

In a few months our organisation was complete; management Committee formed; Ladies Harbour Lights Guild established; funds in the bank contributed by good friends all over Scotland, who were very quick to recognise the great value of the Mission's work amongst Naval and Merchant seamen. It was a very difficult task to procure a suitable site for a Mission, the Naval and Military having priority. However, the L.N.E.R Company, recognising the importance of the *Flying Angel* in the lives of the seamen, offered us an archway inside the dock where we built an up-to-date canteen, equipped it with all the conveniences that space would allow and staffed it with volunteers from our Ladies' Guild. We opened it on 17th June 1940, and hundreds of seamen immediately began to come in a continuous stream, for twelve hours a day, for a refreshing cup of tea and a rest in congenial surroundings.'

By the end of six months, more and more men seeking the amenities which only The Missions to Seamen could provide, and an extension was built in the adjoining archway after driving a doorway through five feet of solid concrete to connect it with the canteen. One end of the new hall was built as a sanctuary, shut off from the hall by folding doors which were opened for church services and closed when the hall was being used for recreational and entertainment purposes. The little Mission under the Arches gave welcome and comfort to many hundreds of survivors who landed cold, wet, hungry and injured . The Methil Station was in a very real sense a haven from which men would go out to battle, fortified and strengthened to the task before them.

The mission was still too small but was self-supporting, and built within four feet of the quayside, with ships lying up under the very windows, it served fifteen thousand cups of tea per month. Every Christmas they had ten days' festivities, commencing on 22nd December and going on until New Year's Eve. Six hundred men were given Christmas dinner and hundreds more turned up to enjoy the entertainment, which included concerts, cinema shows, whist drives and parties.

Before 1939, few people had heard of Methil but during the war, tens of thousands of men visited the Mission beneath the arches at Methil docks. Right on the dock-side, it was just where it was needed for the seven and fifty thousand or so men who, during the war, could drop in just as they were and find a friendly welcome from the Chaplain, his wife and the voluntary helpers. The Chaplain always made a point of seeing ships off and saying goodbye at the pier head whenever possible, but crews of ships joining the convoys in the Firth of Forth often never got ashore at all. The Chaplain would go out to the ships. Belgians, Norwegians, Dutch, Greek, Free French and Poles were all on his visiting list. For some sailors, in a quick turn round, all they saw of Methil was

Levenmouth at War

the docks, the coal tip and the Mission man. In one year, he visited nine hundred and thirty ships.

In a booklet written about the *Flying Angel's* work in Methil, the Chaplain speaks of 'pathetic streams' of shipwrecked men being brought from the sea, wrapped in sacks or tarpaulins, some badly injured. One night two hundred and sixty six men, including a number of Indian seamen, were brought ashore. Sometimes the rescued men had left the port only a few hours before. The clothes they were given did not always fit but were always clean and dry, and no one was turned away without something to wear till their own clothes could be replaced. There were hair raising incidents, for example when one ship came into port with two unexploded bombs aboard.

During the run up to the invasion in 1944, the canteen opened at six thirty in the morning. Some of the women helpers would do over two hours work before setting off for their own place of business, and would return to do another four hours in the evening.

The work of the Seamen's Mission goes on today. With the war in Iraq, ports like Dubai where the convoys for the war were based, found that the seamen not only from the merchant ships but naval personnel were glad to find the facilities offered by the Flying Angel club.

Times are changing though and the quicker turn round of ships and the practice of flying seamen to join their ships means that a very short time is spent in port. Seamen are recruited for a ship from many different countries, mostly low wage, developing countries and a man can find himself as one of a crew say of fifteen all of whom speak a different language. English is the official language on board ships but many men have a very limited understanding of it, enough perhaps to do their job but not enough to engage in conversation. Sometimes a man is on board for eighteen months without a break to go home, so life can be very lonely and the Mission has tried to meet this requirement by providing facilities to enable men to keep in touch with home and family. Wherever possible, someone to speak the language of the seaman is provided so that he can discuss personal problems such as a bereavement at home, dangerous conditions on board, inadequate or non-payment of wages or denial of medical treatment. In fact, justice issues are a growing problem. Crewmen can be left in a hospital, or left abandoned and stranded by companies which run into financial difficulties or who just walk away from their responsibilities.

With the millennium it was decided to change the name from the Mission to Seamen to the Mission to Seafarers since the Society cares for all who earn their living at sea, regardless of their gender, nationality, faith or rank. There are now many specialised ports world wide which have been built long distances from centres of population and these have necessitated building new centres. At present the mission has full time chaplains and/or centres in more than a hundred ports around the world and is represented in some two hundred others where volunteers work part time with seafarers.

The arches at Methil Docks where the Flying Angel was based

Levenmouth at War

ARCHAEOLOGICAL REMAINS

There are very few World War Two relics left in the Levenmouth area, but one of them is an XDO post, that is, an Extended Defence Officers Post, at Swan Brae, on the south side of Methil.

The XDO post has been buried with only the top visible above ground and trees have been planted round it with the intention of concealing the structure. The site was possibly the subject of landscaping works initiated by the former Kirkcaldy District Council, probably in partnership with the Scottish Development Agency, some time in the late 1980s or the early 1990s.

Vandalism was a problem and, to prevent the post being used as a den, landscaping works were implemented to bury the site, thus preventing access to it. Only the roof-top concrete observation turret is now visible above ground, but it is likely that as a reinforced concrete building, this XDO post is as solid and bomb-proof as it was when it was first constructed back in 1939.

As the structure is now almost completely buried, it is difficult from a written description alone to understand how it would have originally appeared. However, as XDO posts were largely built to a standard military pattern, comparison with other similar sites demonstrates approximately what the Methil post would look like if it were to be uncovered.

The general form of these structures is almost always the same, but some were slightly bigger than others, the size being relative to the size of the docks they were protecting and the consequent number of staff they had to house.

Originally, it would have been made from reinforced concrete, about nine foot square and about eight feet high, with an entrance door in its north-east or north-west corner, which would be slightly angled for blast protection. This blast-protected access door is probably the full height of the post. There are probably two elongated loop-holes in the south-east or south west corner, which look out to sea.

On top of the roof, right in the centre, is a smaller concrete turret, cube shaped, about three feet higher than the roof of the building. This roof turret observation point has a small observation embrasure, a loop-hole or a viewing slit, in each of its four faces. To reach this turret from inside, a short iron ladder with four or five rungs, would have been fixed to the floor directly beneath it, high enough to enable a man to climb up the ladder and peer through the turret loop-holes with ease.

The building was probably manned by a detachment of about eight Marines and a commanding naval officer, it is possible that there might have been slightly more or slightly fewer men stationed here but even for eight men, it would have been quite cramped.

This post was necessary because Methil was a marshalling point for convoys during the Second World War, and also controlled access to the Forth Rail Bridge and to the naval base at Rosyth. Methil docks were of considerable strategic importance, so this XDO post was of immense military importance as a link in the integrated defence system of the Forth.

Built in 1939, this command and observation post was situated in an elevated position with commanding views over Methil docks, and all approaches to the docks would originally have been clearly visible from this site. The XDO had two main functions. Following instructions from the nearby observational headquarters, signals were sent using either an Aldis-Lamp or semaphore, ordering all vessels steaming towards or past the docks to halt.

The area covered by the shore guns would have been marked out by two buoys about two miles apart, delineating a sea area known as the 'Methil Docks Roads', any vessel steaming up the Firth of Forth could be required to halt within this area. The Marines based in the XDO post would send a Navy boarding-party out to a vessel in a pilot-boat to investigate.

The second function was to control the detonation of the submerged mines in the underwater minefield laid around the approaches to Methil docks. That is to say, if an unauthorised vessel or attacking enemy ships steamed towards the docks, the naval control officer in the XDO post could detonate specific mines as required to destroy these attacking vessels.

The Pillbox at Wellesley Pit

ROLL OF HONOUR

METHIL WAR MEMORIAL

LTO John Anderson
Stoker Richard Balfour
CH.ENG George T Beed
A.B. John F. Bowers
Stoker John Crabbe
O.S. William Dickson
P.O. James Doig
A.B. John Fraser
A.B. John Hazzard
STWD. John Jones
O.S. John Milligan
P.O.(TEL.) George Mitchell
L.S. Douglas H. Morton
A.B. Alexander B. Murray
A.B. Robert M. Rafferty
Robert Robertson
A.B. John L. Thomson
Samuel B. Waggett
O.S. Felix Walker
A.B. Alexander Wells
O.S. Stanley Westwood
Stoker James Wilson
Air Mech. John McLellan
Wren Margaret H. Gillies
Wren Isabella Hynd
Peter S. Balfour
Raymond Banna
William E. Bird
Arthur Black
Andrew Brown
Lawrence Brown
John Duffy
William Duthie
James S. Elder
Thomas I. Gardner
William Glover

William Gow
Robert Gray
George Jackson jnr
John J. Lynd
Peter R. McBride
William McGrory
Andrew Marshall
William M. Marshall
James Nelson
Walter Scott
Henry Selfridge
John Smith
John O. Suttie
Peter Taylor
James Wall
William Watson
George Weir
David N. Wilson
PTE John B. Robertson
SGT Edward J. Black
TPR William Perrie
TPR Andrew J. Ried
BDR David W. Anderson
GNR James Anderson
GNR Watson Baird
GNR John C. Barclay
BDR Christopher Baxter
GNR David Beedie
GNR Robert Bell
GNR Ninian Carr
GNR Arthur G. Cunningham
GNR P. Currie
GNR Alexander Hay
GNR John B. Kinnear
GNR R. McConnel
GNR Alexander McLeod
GNR William McMurdo
GNR John Marshall
GNR James S. Muir
BDR John G. Ross
GNR Andrew Swinley

GNR Archie Thomson
GNR William R. Wares
GNR E. Westwood
SPR Robert Baird
SPR Chester Gillon
SPR Robert Reid
CPL John Snowball
CFN. Thomas Anderson
GDN. Alexander Beveridge
LCPL. John W. Falls
Robert Gray
George Jackson jnr
John J. Lynd
Peter R. McBride
William McGrory
Andrew Marshall
William M. Marshall
James Nelson
Walter Scott
Henry Selfridge
John Smith
John O. Suttie
GDN. David Morrison
GDN. Archibald S.S. Peggie
CPL. John Skinner
PTE. Thomas J. Storrar
FSLR. Robert Williams
PTE. Dennis O'Donnell
FSLR. Leslie G. Goddard
SGT. Alexander Graham
CPL. John Melville
PTE. James B. Moyes
SGT. Robert S. Swan
SGT. A.G. Brewster
CPL. James Wilson
CPL. Alexander S. Arnott
PTE. James Porter
LIEUT. Alfred Lagergren
PTE. Euphemia H. White
SGT PIL. David S. Allan
SGT. William Boyle

F/O. Peter A. Bradley
Cadet Thomas W. Calderhead
F/SGT. Thomas D. Cant
CPL. Thomas Davidson
F/SGT. James Dick
SGT. OBS. Oliver W. Dumbreck
P/O Alex R. Edgar D.F.M
F/SGT. Andrew Gillies
SGT/PIL. Robert A. Jerrit
F/SGT. Lawrence Lawson
F/SGT. John McKelvie
CPL. Robert N. Meldrum
F/O. Robert Moyes
P/O. Archibald Orr
SGT. Michael N. Reilly
A.C.2 James Ross
P/O. Ronald M. Simpson
SGT. Andrew Thomson
L.A.C. Thomas S. Wallace
F/SGT. Edwin Watson
PTE. Peter McGovern
Robert Birrell
George Irvine
George Jensen
Robert Jensen
Joe Kinnear
William Kinnear
John Thomson
Henry Walton
Colin Webster
Henry Wilkie
James Wilkie
L/CPL. George Hunter
R.F.N. Robert A. Watters
Alexander Williams
PTE. Alexander Foster
PTE. Archibald Black
PTE. James Chalmers
PTE. Charles A. Clark
L/SGT. John B. Coote
L/CPL. William C. Erskine

Levenmouth at War

PTE. James Fairfull
PTE. James Ford
L/CPL. George D. Gorrie M.M.
PTE. Alex A. Henderson
PTE. James S. McBride
PTE. George C. MacKay
PTE. Robert W. McKenzie
Thomas McWilliams
C.S.M Jack Morrison
PTE. George Mortimer
PTE. Robert Muirhead
CPL. Thomas Murray
DRMR. Thomas Purvis
PTE. Hugh Rae
PTE. Thomas Reilly
C.S.M John W. Simpson
PTE. John R. Staig
SGT. Austin Strachen
L/CPL. Daniel L. Thomson
L/CPL. George Todd
PTE. Robert W. Walton
SGT. William N.S. Watson
PTE. John M.B. Younger
PTE. Ronald C.S. Scheffler
PTE. Robert Adams
PTE. William Skinner
SPL. William H. Dunsmuir
PTE. George Baird
PTE. James M. Bayne
PTE. Alexander Fraser
CPL. David Keddie
DVR. John D.H. Johnstone
PTE. John R. Johnstone
PTE. James Little
DVR. Walter B. Peggie

LEVEN WAR MEMORIAL

P.O William W. Beveridge
A.B. Henry B. Blyth
STO.1ST.C. Robert Cheape
A.B. John B. Cowper
CPL. James Wilson
CPL. William H. Brand
Chief Eng'r. Randolph F.D. Campbell
Trimmer James I.P. Duff
Asst. Eng'r. George Finlay
Asst. Cook John B. Gartshore
Stoker Alexander S. Herd
Jnr Eng'r. George H. Smith
Chief Officer William Smith
TPR. John Duncan
TPR. John Warrender
L.CPL. John Cumming
TPR. Andrew J. Reid
GNR. Alexander Anderson
GNR. George H. Birrell
B.S.M. James B.G. Birrell
DVR. James Bisset
GNR. David G. Blackwood
L.BDR. Robert A. Doig
GNR. Owen Duffy
GNR. Charles L. Graham
BDR. James W. Hastie
GNR. Edward J. Minford
GNR. Robert D. McConnell
CAPT. J. Patrick O. Russell
BDR. Alex. R. Smith B.E.M.
L.BDR. John R. Thomson
BDR. James R. Watt
SIG. Walter White
CPL. William I. Christie
L.CPL. John W. Falls
GDSM. Archibald Shanks
PTE. John S. Duff
PTE. Albert S. Falconer
LT. John S. Middlemass

Levenmouth at War

DRMR. Alan M. Smith
L.CPL. William D. Ross
PTE. Alexander Wilson
RFN. William C. Laing
PTE. Andrew W. Brown
PTE. Robert E.A. Doig
PTE. Thomas T. Doig
SGT. Thomas Kirkcaldy
PTE. Frank Rankin
PTE. Thomas White
CPL. Adam C. McLuckie
PTE. Thomas Penman
PTE. Thomas S. Robertson
DVR. Thomas P. W. Dawson
CAPT. A. Douglas Reid
DVR. James G. Young
LT. David W. Bell
CPL. William H. Ritchie
CPL. James F. Speed
PTE. Alexander J. Clacher
PTE. John L. Gordon
STG.W.O.A.G. James Adam
SGT.WO.A.G. Robert E. Burt
L.A.C. William Chalmers
SGT. NAV'R. Alexander H. Croll
L.A.C.W. Elizabeth S. Dempster
F.O. James R. Ferguson
SGT.W.O.A.G. William N. Forrester
L.A.C. James S. Gardner
SGT.GNR. George C. Hutton
SGT.SIG'R Thomas Morris
SGT.NAV'R. John S. Porter
SGT.A.G. David E. Robertson
F/LT. George Russell D.F.C.
F.O. James C. Stevenson D.F.C.
L.A.C. Peter Thomson
A.C.I Joseph Wilson
F.SGT.ENG'R. George D. Wright

KENNOWAY WAR MEMORIAL

Robert Armstrong
William Black
Andrew Brown
Mitchell Collins
Gordon Condie
Jack Greig
Andrew McDonald
Thomas McLennan
Hugh Orr
David Ramsay
Douglas Robertson

COALTOWN OF WEMYSS WAR MEMORIAL

Robert Anderson
John Clark
William Givens
Charles Hill
John McLaren
James Milne
William Muirhead

WEST WAR MEMORIAL

Corporal David Brown
Seaman James J. Henderson
Seaman Peter Herd
Seaman Robert Smart
Sapper Robert T. Walker
Sergeant David P. Westwater

EAST WEMYSS WAR MEMORIAL

T. Adams
W. Adamson
W. Berry
D. Dewar
R.W. Drummond

H.J. Evans
I.H. Forbes
J. Fotheringham
R.L. Givens
C. Gorrie M.M.
T. Greenhill
J. Johnston
A. Logie
L. McDonald
J.D. McLaren
C. Mearns
D.R. Mowett
P. Murray
I. Prentice
J. Robertson
A. Shields
W. Simpson
C. Skinner
W.I. Smith
A.J.F. Walker
W. Welsh
W.W. Williamson
R. Young

WINDYGATES WAR MEMORIAL

James D. Drysdale
Robert Duff
Robert Duff
James S. Elder
Thomas T.L. Hastie
David Haig
Robert King
Thomas M. McLennan
Isaac L. Murdoch
James Petrie
Alexander Rankine
Robert K. Wardlaw
Robert Wilkie
Jack Wilson
Thomas Wilson

Levenmouth at War

PICTURE ACKNOWLEDGEMENT

Pictures are reproduced by kind permission of the following:
Kirkcaldy Museum and Art Gallery - front cover, 1, 71, 118,
131, 140, 153, 157, 182
Janet Ramsay – 108, 113, 114
Mary Bell -142, 144
Jimmy Laird – 147
Desrenee Irvine – 61, 159, 166
Jim Hamilton - 179

ABOUT THE AUTHOR

Lillian King is a graduate of Edinburgh University. Most of her career has been in Adult Education and she is now a part time tutor with the WEA. Her particular interests are railways, mining and women's history. She has edited several books, including *Dugs, Doos and Dancing, Expendable,* and *In Search of the Scottish Wildcat,* as well as a number of anthologies, and had articles in a variety of publications including The Scotsman, The Scots Magazine and The Times Educational Supplement.
Previous books include:

A Railway Childhood,
The Last Station,
Thornton Railway Days
Famous Women of Fife
Building The Bridge
Sair, Sair Wark, Women and Mining in Scotland
That's Entertainment, 100 Years of Dunfermline
Opera House